Instant
Dutch

by

Dorothy Thomas & Marilyn Zack-Depraetere

Illustrated by

apropos design

dot publications

Marilyn Zack-Depraetere writes:

When I moved from Flanders to Newcastle upon Tyne in 1988, I never thought I'd teach Dutch again. Wrong ... thirteen years later we are still going strong with two classes full of very enthusiastic students, many of whom have become very good friends.

I would like to thank all of them who have made teaching my mother tongue in England such a pleasure.

Dorothy Thomas:

Coming to Dutch the long way round after teaching another Germanic language, Norwegian, it has been fascinating to see how they all fit together – and particularly enjoyable working with such a lively and agreeable colleague.

Published by dot Publications, 54a Haig Avenue, Whitley Bay NE25 8JD

First published 2001
Copyright © D M Thomas 2001

ISBN 1 871086 10 8

Typeset by Robographics, Glasgow
Printed in the UK by Bell & Bain Ltd, Glasgow

Nederland - the Netherlands
België - Belgium   *(Vlaanderen* - Flanders)

Noordzee

Waddenzee

IJsselmeer

Groningen
Leeuwarden

NEDERLAND

Zwolle

Haarlem
Amsterdam
Den Haag
Rotterdam
Utrecht
Arnhem
Nijmegen

IJssel

Waal

Rijn

DUITSLAND
(GERMANY)

Tilburg
Eindhoven

Maas

Antwerpen

Oostende
Brugge   Gent

BELGIË

Schelde

Brussel

Maastricht
Luik

Aken
(Aachen)

Rijssel (Lille)

FRANKRIJK
(FRANCE)

LUXEMBURG

4 *Contents*

Using this book

Even if you have never learned another language before, this book will help you to get by, so you can get whatever you need or wherever you want to go.

Right at the back are some **basic phrases**, covering such essentials as *yes, no, please, thank you, I don't understand* - and *help!*

Just before this, on p. 131, is a list of **numbers** from 0 to a million. It's worth learning these, as numbers are a vital part of a language and will make it much easier to buy things or make arrangements. You will also need numbers for using the **phone**, p. 53, and telling the **time**, p. 55.

The book is divided into a series of typical situations, showing the words you need with an idea of the replies you are likely to hear. Follow the speech guide under each picture. The guide to **sounds** on p. 6 will help you pronounce things correctly.

To find a particular item, the easiest way is to look it up in the **dictionary/index** (Dutch p. 98, English p. 112).

Food: there is a comprehensive guide to Dutch menu terms on pp. 30-37, with a few English ones at the end (all items are also in the dictionary). Both English and Dutch names are shown in the shopping section: **meat** p. 40, **fish** p. 41, **fruit and vegetables** pp. 42-43 and **groceries** p. 44.

If you would like to know more about the nuts and bolts of the language, there is a brief **grammatical** section on pp. 96-97.

Guess! Many words are the same in both Dutch and English - or very similar - so if you don't know what a particular word is, have a guess!

Enjoy yourself, have a good trip, and - ***Prettige reis!***

Dutch sounds

Conveying the sounds of one language in those of another is notoriously difficult, but this will help you to produce a rough approximation.

Stress This is usually on the first syllable (second after the prefixes *be-, er-, ge-, her-, ont-, ver-*). The letters to be stressed are shown in **heavy** type (underlined in the dictionary). Some words are split by a hyphen to make them easier to read and get the stress in the right place: pronounce them as one word, with no gaps.

Vowels (Long/short vowels: see p.96)

		Example	*Sounded*
e (unstressed), **-ijk**, **-ig** like *a* in china		de, hartelijk, twintig	*duh, -lukk, -tukh*
a	between *a* in mat and *u* in cut	van	*van*
aa	like *a* in father	laat	*laat*
aai	*aa + ee*	draai	*dry*
e	like *e* in bet	met	*met*
ee	like *a* in late	heeft	*hayft*
eeu	*ay*, followed quickly by *uw* or *oo* or	sneeuw	***snay**-(uw)*
ei, ij	like *ay* in may	trein, vrij	*trayn, vray*
eu	like *ur* in fur, but without the *r*	sleutel	***slurt**el*
i	like *i* in pin	ik	*ik*
ie	like *ee* in beetroot	biet	*beet*
ieu	same sound as *ew* in new	nieuw	*new*
o	like *o* as in coffee	koffie	*koffee*
oe	like *oo* as in moon	hoe	*hoo*
oei	*oo + ee*	moeite	***moo**-eetuh*
oo	like *oa* as in boat	boot	*boat*
ooi	like *oa* as in road, plus *ee*	mooi	***moh**-ee*
ou	like *o* in cold, plus *oo*	koud, blauw	*kowt, bl-ow*
u	like a short uw	bus	*buwss*
uu	like Scots or French *u*, or German *ü*	u	*oo*
ui	like *uh* followed very quickly by *oo*	uit	*uh(oo)t*

Consonants

b, d	are pronounced *p, t* at the end of a word	heb, hoed	*hep, hoot*
ch, g	the guttural sound of *ch* in loch	acht, goed	*akht, khoot*
ge	(French loan words only) like *s* in measure	asperges	*ass**pairz**huss*
j	like *y* in yes; occasionally like *s* in measure	ja; jam	*ya; zhem*
nj	like *ni* in onion	oranje	*or-**an**yuh*
sch	*s + ch* sound above	schaar	*s'kh/ s'haar*
	(but *-isch* pronounced *-iss*)		
sj	like *sh* in she	sjaal	*shaal*
th	like *t* in tea	thee	*tay*
tje	a gentle *chuh* or *tyuh*	katje	*katyuh*
w	like *v*, but bottom lip only touches top teeth lightly	wat	*vat*

Booking accommodation

Geachte Heer, Mevrouw,   Dear Sir or Madam,

Hotels

Kan ik reserveren I should like to book	*een eenpersoonskamer* a single room	*twee eenpersoonskamers* two single rooms
een/twee one/two	*tweepersoonskamers* double rooms	*een familiekamer* a family room
met bad/douche with bath/shower	*voor ... nachten* for ... nights	*van ... tot ...* from ... to ...

Camping

Kan ik een kampplaats (met elektriciteitsvoorziening) bij u reserveren. Het liefst uit de zon.

I should like to book a pitch (with electricity) on your campsite, in the shade if possible.

We zouden ... nachten blijven,   *van ... tot ...*
We wish to stay ... nights,   from ... to ...

We beschikken over   *een auto/ een caravan/ een kampeerauto*
We have   a car/ a caravan/ a motor caravan

en   *een grote/kleine tent (met voortent).*
and   a large/small tent (with awning).

*   *   *

Heeft u ook faciliteiten voor andersvaliden?
Have you any facilities for the disabled?

Ik heb een rolstoel.   *Ik wil een kamer op de benedenverdieping.*
I use a wheelchair.   I'd like a room on the ground floor.

*   *   *

We reizen met   *... volwassenen en*   *... kind/kinderen van ... jaar oud.*
We shall be   ... adults and   ... child/children aged ...

Kunt u   me/ons uw tarieven toesturen?
Please let me/us know your rates.

Hoeveel bedraagt het voorschot voor   *de kamer/kamers (de kampplaats)?*
How much deposit is required to book   the room/rooms   (the pitch)?

Hoogachtend,
Yours faithfully,

Hotels

Dutch and Belgian hotels quote prices per room, not per person. Breakfast is usually included but not always, so it is advisable to check (p.13). It is quite usual to inspect the room first - and to refuse if you don't like it. **Kamers/Kamers vrij** - 'Rooms available'.

1. *Dakh! (Hooyuh **mor**khuh/ hooyuh **midd**akh).*
   Hello! (Good morning/ good afternoon).

2. *Hooyuh **mor**khuh (hooyuh **midd**akh).*
   Good morning (good afternoon).

3. *Mayn **naam** iss ... Ik hep 'n **kaa**mer khe**ray**zer-**vayrt** vor van-**nakht**.*
   My name is ... I've booked a room for tonight.

4. *Ya, **kaa**mer **teen**.*
   Oh yes, it's room 10.

5. *Makh-ik oo (**pass**port/ eedenty-**tayts** kaart), ashoo-**bleeft**?*
   *Kuntoo **heer** ayvuh **tay**kunn-uh?*
   Could I have your (passport/ identity card), please? Please sign here.

1. *Vaar kannik mayn ow-toh par-**kay**ruh?*
   Where can I park?

2. *Vat-iss oo **ken**tay-kuh nummer?*
   What is your registration number?

een nacht *ayn nakht* a/one night		**twee nachten** *tvay nakhtuh* two nights	

een week
ayn vayk a/one week

If you haven't booked

1. Goedenavond. Heeft u een kamer vrij?

2. Jazeker. Voor hoeveel personen?

3. Voor één persoon (twee personen), en één kind (twee kinderen).

4. Goed. Voor hoelang?

5. Voor (één nacht/ één week).

1. *Hooyuh **aa**vont. Hayft-oo 'n **kaa**mer **vray**?*
   Good evening. Have you a room available?

2. *Ya-**zay**ker. Vor hoo-vayl per-**soan**uh?*
   Certainly. How many for?

3. *Vor **ayn** per-**soan** (tvay per-**soan**uh), en ayn kint (tvay **kind**eruh).*
   For one person (two ...), and one child (two children).

4. *Khoot. Vor **hoo**-lang?*
   Fine. How long for?

5. *Vor (ayn nakht/ ayn vayk).*
   For (one night/ a week).

Sorry, maar we zijn volgeboekt.
...*maar **vuzz**ayn **vol**khuh-bookt.*
Sorry, we're full.

Is er een ander hotel in de buurt?
*Isser 'n **ander** ho**tel** induh **buwrt**?*
Is there another hotel nearby?

Volgeboekt - it's full

In towns the Tourist Office will help you find a room (all speak English). Look for **VVV** in the Netherlands, in Belgium **Het bureau voor toerisme**.

2. Een tweepersoonskamer (en een familiekamer).

4. Met douche en W.C.

5. Kunnen we over een extra bed beschikken? (een kinderbedje)

1. Wilt u een kamer voor één persoon of voor twee personen?

3. Met bad of douche en W.C.?

1. *Viltoo 'n **kaa**mer vor **ayn** per-**soan** off vor **tvay** per-**soan**uh?*
   Would you like a single room or a double?

2. *'N **tvay** per-**soan**ss **kaa**mer (en 'n fam-**ee**ly **kaa**mer).*
   A double room (and a family room).

3. *__Met__ bat off doosh en vay-**say**?*
   With bath or shower and toilet?

4. *__Met__ doosh en vay-**say**.*
   With shower and W.C.

5. *__Kunn__uh-vuh over 'n **ex**tra bet bus-**hikk**uh? ('n **kin**der bet-yuh)*
   Could we have an extra bed, please? (a child's bed)

een bed voor één persoon
*'n bet vor **ayn** per-**soan***
a single bed

een tweepersoonsbed
*'n **tvay** per-**soan**ss bet*
a double bed

twee eenpersoonsbedden
*tvay **ayn** per-**soan**ss bedduh*
twin beds

de douche
duh doosh
the shower

het bad
t(uh) bat
the bath

de W.C.
*duh vay-**say***
the lavatory

Talking to staff: pp.14, 15

1. *Ya, vuh **hebb**uh 'n **kaa**mer **vray**.*
   Yes, we have a room available.

2. *Khoot. Vat **kost** dee?*
   Good. How much is it?

3. *Hut **iss** ... per **nakht**.*
   It's ... a night.

4. *Khoot. Ik **naym** duh **kaa**mer.*
   Fine, I'll take it.

5. *Makh-ik oo **naam** en oo (**pass**port/ eedenty-**tayts**kaart), ashoo-**bleeft**?*
   Good. Could I have your name, please, and your (passport/ identity card)?

6. *Zo. Mayn **naam** iss ...*
   Here you are. My name is ...

7. *Kuntoo **heer** ayvuh **tay**kunnuh?*
   Could you sign here, please?

8. *Dankoo. **Heer** iss oo **slur**tel.*
   Thank you. Here is your key.

Mag ik mijn sleutel, alsjeblieft? Kamer achttien.
*Makh-ik mayn **slur**tel, ashoo-**bleeft**? **Kaa**mer **akh**teen.*
Could I have my key, please? Room 18.

1. Mag ik de kamer even zien?
2. Ja, natuurlijk.
3. Ik neem de kamer.
6. Het spijt me, meneer...
4. De kamer is te duur. (Er is te veel lawaai.)
5. Heeft u ook een kamer die (goedkoper/stiller) is?

1. *Makh-ik duh **kaa**mer **ay**vuh zeen?*
   Can I see the room?

2. *Ya, nat-**uwr**lukk.*
   Yes, of course.

3. *Ik **naym** duh **kaa**mer.*
   I'll take it.

4. *Duh **kaa**mer iss tuh-**duwr**. (Er **iss** tuh-**vayl** lav-**eye**).*
   The room is too expensive. (It's too noisy.)

5. *Hayft-oo oak 'n **kaa**mer dee (khoot-**koap**er/ stiller) iss?*
   Have you a (cheaper/quieter) room?

6. *Hut **spayt**muh, munn-**ayr**...*
   I'm sorry, sir...

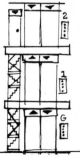

de eerste*/tweede verdieping
*duh **ayr**stuh/**tvay**duh ver-**deep**ing*
the first/second floor

de benedenverdieping
*duh bun-**ay**duh ver-**deep**ing*
the ground floor

de lift
duh lift
the lift

*eerste may also be ground floor

1. Mag ik een kamer op de benedenverdieping?

2. Is hier een lift?

1. *Makh-ik 'n **kaa**mer opduh bun-**ay**duh ver-**deep**ing?*
   Could I have a room on the ground floor, please?

2. ***Iss** heer 'n **lift**?*
   Is there a lift?

1. *Iss hut ont-**bayt in**buh-khraypuh?*
   Is breakfast included?

2. *Ont-**bayt** iss (**ex**kloo-seef/ **in**kloo-seef).*
   Breakfast is (extra/included).

3. *Hoo-laat ser-**vayrt**oo (ont-**bayt**/ luwnsh/ hut **aa**vont-maal)?*
   When do you serve (breakfast/ lunch/ dinner)?

4. *Van **hallf** akht tot **teen** uwr.*
   From 7*.30 to 10.   *Time p.55 (7.30 = half <u>acht</u>)

1. *Makh-ik duh **ray**ken-ing, ashoo-**bleeft**?*
   Could I have the bill, please?

2. *Kannik buh-**taal**uh met (**rayss**-sheks/ kred-**it** kaart)?*
   Can I pay by (traveller's cheque/ credit card)?

3. *Makh-ik 'n **bonnet**-yuh, ashoo-**bleeft**?*
   Could I have a receipt, please?

4. ***Hartuh**-luk dank. Tot seenss.*
   Thanks for everything. Goodbye.

> *Alles inbegrepen/*
> *BTW inbegrepen*
> All taxes included

de schoorsteen
duh s'horstayn
the Chimney

de deur
duh dur
the Door

de goot
duh khoat
the Drain

de regenpijp
duh raykhen payp
the Drainpipe

de afsluiting
duh afsluh(oo)-ting
the Fence

de tuin
duh tuh(oo)n
the Garden

de sleutels
duh slurtels
the Keys

een ladder
'n ladder
a Ladder

het slot
hut slot
the Lock

het dak
hut dak
the Roof

de sceptische put
duh septisser put
the Septic Tank

een tegel
'n taykhel
a Tile

de muur
duh muwr
the Wall

het venster
hut venster
the Window

General matters

1. Pardon, ik zoek ...
   *Per-**don**, ik **zook** ...*
      Excuse me, I'm looking for ...

2. Waar woont (hij/zij)?
   Vaar voant (hay/zay)?
      Where does (he/she) live?

3. Mag ik een extra (deken), alsjeblieft?
   *Makh-ik 'n extra (**day**kuh), ashoo-**bleeft**?*
      Could I have an extra (blanket), please?

4. Wanneer is de vuilnisomhaling?
   *Van-**ayr** iss duh **vuh**(oo)l-niss **om**haal-ing?*
      When is the rubbish collected?

5. Kan ik ... lenen, alsjeblieft?
   *Kannik ... **lay**nuh, ashoo-**bleeft**?*
      Can I borrow ... please?

Thanks

Hartelijk dank voor uw hulp. Ik ben u erg dankbaar.
***Har**tuh-luk dank vor oo **hulp**. Ik ben oo **airkh dank**bar.*
      Thanks for your help. I'm extremely grateful.

Problems

een aannemer
*'n **aan**-naymer*
a Builder

een timmerman
*'n **timmer**-man*
a Carpenter

een elektricien
*'n aylektriss-**yeng***
an Electrician

een loodgieter
*'n **loat** kheeter*
a Plumber

een schilder/behanger
*'n s'**hilder**/ buh-**hang**er*
a Decorator

... **is geblokkeerd**
*iss khublokk-**ayrt***
... is Blocked

... **is gebroken**
*iss khuh-**broak**uh*
... is Broken

... **is los gekomen**
*iss **loss** khuh-**koam**uh*
... has Come Off

... **is gebarsten**
*iss khuh-**barst**uh*
... is Cracked

... **lekt**
lekt
... is Leaking

... **is los**
iss loss
... is Loose

... **werkt niet**
*vairkt **neet***
... doesn't Work

1. Kunt u me tonen hoe dit werkt?
   ***Kun**toomuh **toan**uh hoo dit **vairkt**?*
   Can you show me how this works?

2. Het dak lekt.
   *Hut **dak** lekt.*
   The roof is leaking.

3. Kunt u dit repareren?
   *Kuntoo dit raypa-**ray**ruh?*
   Can you mend it?

4. Hoe lang gaat dat duren?
   *Hoo-lang **khaat** dat **duw**ruh?*
   How long will it take?

5. Wat gaat dat kosten?
   *Vat **khaat** dat **kost**uh?*
   What will it cost?

6. Kunt u een ... aanbevelen?
   *Kuntoo 'n ... **aan**buh-vayluh?*
   Can you recommend a ...?

Wanneer kunt u dat doen?
*Van-**ayr** kuntoo dat **doon**?*
When can you do it?

When? – wanneer? – van-ayr?

Het hoeft niet per se (vandaag/nu). (Morgen/later) is OK.
*Hut **hooft** neet per-**say** (van-**daakh**/nuw). Morkher/laater) iss **OK**.*
It doesn't need to be done (today/now). (Tomorrow/later) will be OK.

The living room – *de woonkamer* – *voan kaamer*

een leunstoel	het plafond	de kast	de gordijnen	de gordijnstang
*'n **lurn**stool*	*hut plaff-**ont***	*duh kast*	*duh khor-**dayn**uh*	*duh khor**dayn** stang*
an Armchair	the Ceiling	the Cupboard	the Curtains	the Curtain Rail

de haard	de vloer	de luiken	de trap	het venster
duh haart	*duh vlor*	*duh **luh**(oo)-kuh*	*duh trap*	*hut venster*
the Fireplace	the Floor	the Shutters	the Stairs	the Window

The bedroom – *de slaapkamer* – *slaap kaamer*

het bed	de dekens	het dekbed	de lamp	de verlichting
hut bet	*duh **day**kuss*	*hut **dek**bet*	*duh lamp*	*duh ver-**likht**ing*
the Bed	the Blankets	the Eiderdown	a Lamp	the Light

een gloeilamp	een hoofdkussen	de kussensloop	de lakens
*'n **khloo**-ee lamp*	*'n **hoaft** kussuh*	*duh **kuss**usloap*	*duh **laak**enss*
a Light Bulb	a Pillow	the Pillowcase	the Sheets

het bad
hut bat
the Bath

de douche
duh doosh
the Shower

de stekker voor het **scheerapparaat**
*duh stekker vor-hut s'**hayr** appa-**raat***
the Shaving Point

een handdoek
*'n **han**-dook*
a Towel

de spiegel
*duh **spee**khel*
the Mirror

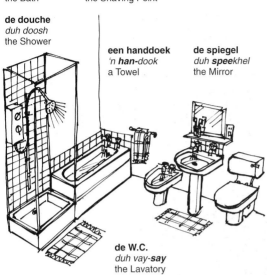

de W.C.
*duh vay-**say***
the Lavatory

de kraan
duh kraan
the Tap/Faucet

de wastafel
*duh **vass** taafel*
the Washbasin

de boiler
duh 'boiler'
the Boiler

de centrale verwarming
*sun-**traa**luh ver-**var**ming*
the Central Heating

een zekering
*'n **zayk**ering*
a Fuse

de elektriciteitskast
*duh **ay**lektrisi-**tayts**kast*
the Fuse Box

een gasfles
*'n **khass** fless*
a Gas Bottle

de meter
duh mayter
the Meter

het gaslichtje
*hut **khass** likh-yuh*
the Pilot Light

de pijp
duh payp
the Pipe

de hoofdkraan
*duh **hoaft** kraan*
the Stopcock

de schakelaar
*duh s'**haak**uh-laar*
the Light Switch

de stekker
duh stekker
the (electric) Plug

het stopcontact
*hut **stop** kon-**takt***
the Socket

warm en (koud) water
varm en (kowt) vaater
hot and (cold) Water

de water-verwarmer
*duh vaater ver-**varm**er*
the Water Heater

Gas/electrics/plumbing

Dicht Off
Open On

1. Er is een (gas/water) lek.
   *Er **iss** 'n (khass/vaater) lek.*
   There's a (gas/water) leak.

2. Draai de hoofdkraan van het (gas/water) dicht.
   *Dry duh **hoaft** kraan van-hut (khass/vaater) **dikht**.*
   Turn the (gas/water) off.

3. De gastank is leeg.
   *Duh **khass**-tank iss **laykh**.*
   The gas has run out.

4. Er is geen (warm) water.
   *Er iss **khayn** (varm) vaater.*
   There's no (hot) water.

5. Is de elektriciteit inbegrepen?
   *Iss-duh **ay**lektrisi-**tayt in**buh-khraypuh?*
   Is electricity included?

Appliances

de vaatwasmachine
duh vaatvass
mash-eenuh
the Dishwasher

de vrieskast
duh vreess-kast
the Freezer

de ijskast
duh ayss-kast
the Fridge

een haardroger
'n haar-droakher
a Hair Dryer

een strijkijzer
'n strayk-ayzer
an Iron

de magnetron
duh makhnay-tron
the Microwave

het fornuis
hut forn-uh(oo)ss
the Stove

de televisie
duh taylay-veezee
the TV

de TV-antenne
duh t... v... an-tennuh
the TV Aerial

de stofzuiger
duh stof zuh(oo)-kher
the Vacuum Cleaner

de video
duh viddayo
the Video

de wasmachine
duh vass mash-eenuh
the Washing Machine

het vuilnis/de afval
vuh(oo)l-niss/ afval
the Rubbish/Trash

een pan
'n pan
a Saucepan

een schotel
'n s'hoatel
a Saucer

de gootsteen
duh khoat-stayn
the Sink

een lepel
'n laypel
a Spoon

Cutlery, utensils, etc.

een kommetje
'n kommet-yuh
a Bowl

een stoel
'n stool
a Chair

de koffiepot/theepot
duh coffeepot/taypot
the Coffeepot/Teapot

een kopje
'n kop-yuh
a Cup

een vuilnisblik en borstel
vuh(oo)l-nisblikk en borstel
a Dustpan and Brush

een dweil
'n d(uh)vayl
a Floorcloth

een vork
'n vork
a Fork

een braadpan
'n braat pan
a Frying Pan

een glas
'n hlass
a Glass

een kan
'n kan
a Jug

een mes
'n mess
a Knife

een beker
'n bayker
a Mug

de tafel	**een theelepeltje**	**een keukenhanddoek**	**een bord**
duh taafel	*'n tay laypelt-yuh*	*'n kurken han-dook*	*'n bort*
the Table	a Teaspoon	a Tea Towel	a Plate

Pardon, is hier een camping in de buurt?
*Per-**don**, **iss** heer 'n camping induh **buwrt**?*
Excuse me, is there a campsite near here?

2. Hoe lang wilt u blijven?

4. Met hoeveel personen zijn jullie?

1. Heeft u een plaats voor een (tent/ caravan/ kampeerauto)?

3. Eén nacht (twee nachten/ een week).

5. Eén volwassene en één kind.
(twee volwassenen/ drie kinderen)

6. Wilt u ook aansluiting op de elektriciteit?

7. Is elektriciteit inbegrepen?

1. *Hayft-oo 'n **plaats** vor 'n (tent/ cara-**van**/ kam-**payr ow**-toh)?*
   Have you a pitch for a (tent/ caravan/ motor caravan)?

2. *Hoo-lang viltoo **blay**vuh?*
   How long would you like to stay?

3. ***Ayn** nakht (**tvay** nakhtuh/ ayn vayk).*
   One night (two nights/ a week).

4. *Met hoo-vayl per-**soan**uh zayn **yew**lee?*
   How many are you?

5. ***Ayn** vol-**vass**enuh en **ayn** kint.*
   *(tvay vol-**vass**enuh/ dree **kin**deruh)*
   One person and one child.
   (two people/ three children)

een fles (propaan)gas
*'n fless (pro-**paan**) khass*
a bottle of (propane) gas

6. *Viltoo oak **aan**sluh(oo)-ting opduh **ay**lektrisi-**tayt**?*
   Would you like electricity?

7. *Iss **ay**lektrisi-**tayt in**buh-khraypuh?*
   Is electricity included?

1. **Vat** kost hut per **nakht**?
   How much is it per night?

2. **Dat**-iss dan ... Hayft-oo 'n kam-**payr karn**ay?
   That will be ... Have you a camping carnet?

3. Van-**ayr** vort duh **slakh**-boom khuh-**sloat**uh?
   What time do you close the barrier in the evening?

4. Om **hallf** elf.
   At 10*.30.

*Time p.55 (10.30 = half *elf*)

Youth Hostel

de jeugdherberg   **de huisbewaarder**
yukhd her-**bairkh**   *huh*(oo)ss buh-**var**der
the Youth Hostel   the Warden

1. Hooyuh **dakh**, hayft-oo **plaats** vor van-**nakht**?
   Hello, have you any beds for tonight?

2. Vor hoo-vayl **nakht**uh?
   For how many nights?

3. **Ayn** nakht (**tvay** nakhtuh).
   Heer iss mun **lit**kaart.
   One night (two nights).
   Here's my membership card.

4. Hayft-oo oak 'n (**laak**un-zak/ **slaap**zak)?
   Have you a (sheet bag/sleeping bag)?

Meals:
> *het ontbijt* – substantial breakfast
> *de lunch* – lunch, 12 - 2pm
> *het diner/avondmaal* – evening meal, 6 - 9, possibly 10pm

Menu: *de menukaart* or *de spijskaart*

de dagschotel: dish of the day
koffietafel: light lunch of cold meat, cheese, tea or coffee

eetcafé: usually serves both lunch and evening meal
bruin or *brown café:* drinks, light snacks; ('brown' from the tobacco-flavoured decor)
tea-room: coffee, tea and cakes
koffieshop: as above; sometimes soft drugs

Fast food: *belegde broodjes* - filled rolls, *frites* or *patat* - chips *(met* with mayonnaise, *zonder* salted), *kroketten* - meat or fish rissoles, *maatjesharing* - raw herring with onions, *pannenkoeken* - pancakes, *poffertjes* - fritters, *shoarma* - kebabs, *stroopwafels* - waffels with syrup, *uitsmijter* - bread topped with fried eggs, cheese or ham.

Tipping: optional, though 10-15% often anticipated. Small amounts: round up to nearest whole number. *BTW en bediening inbegrepen* - sales tax and service included.

Basics

Een ... alsjeblieft.	**Wilt u iets anders?**	**Mag ik... de rekening?**
ayn ... ashoo-__bleeft__	*viltoo eets __anderss__?*	*makh-ik... duh __ray__kening?*
A ... please.	Would you like anything else?	May I have... the bill, please?

Proost!	**Smakelijk!**	**Ik heb honger/dorst**
proast!	*__smaak__uh-luk!*	*ik hep hoong-er/dorst*
Cheers!	Enjoy your meal!	I'm hungry/thirsty

een mes	**een vork**	**een lepel**	**een glas**	**een kopje**
'n mess	*'n vork*	*'n __layp__ul*	*'n hlass*	*'n kop-yuh*
a Knife	a Fork	a Spoon	a Glass	a Cup

Ordering drinks and snacks

> 1. Dag, zegt u het maar?
>
> 4. We hebben broodjes (ham) en <u>kaas</u>.
>
> 2. Twee koffies, een milkshake, en een appelsap alsjeblieft.
>
> 3. Wat voor broodjes heeft u?

1. *Dakh, **zekht**-oo hut **maar**?*
   Hello, what would you like?

2. *Tvay koffees, 'n **milk**shake, en 'n **app**elsap, ashoo-**bleeft**.*
   Two coffees, a milkshake, and an apple juice, please.

3. *Vatfor **broat**-yuss hayft-oo?*
   What kind of rolls have you got?

4. *Vuh hebbuh broat-yuss **(ham)** en <u>**kaass**</u>.*
   We have (ham) and <u>cheese</u> rolls.

een koffie/decafé
*'n koffee/**day**-kaffay*
a Coffee/Decaffeinated ~

een thee
'n tay
a Tea

met citroen/melk/ijs
*met sit-**roon**/melk/ayss*
with Lemon/Milk/Ice

een sinaasappelsap
*'n **sin**uss-**app**elsap*
an Orange Juice

frites/patat
*free**tuh**/pat-**aat***
Chips/Fries
(met - with Mayonnaise)

(erwten) soep
(airvtuh) soop
(Pea) Soup

een uitsmijter
*'n **uh**(oo)t smayter*
Fried Egg, Cheese/
Ham on Bread

een glas water/wijn
*'n hlass **vaa**ter/vayn*
a Glass of Water/Wine (p.29)

een bier
'n beer
a Beer

een cola/cola light
*'n cola/cola **light***
a Coke/Diet Coke

1. *Hoo **hayt** deet?*
   What's that called?

2. *Khayft-oo muh-**mar** vat-van **dee**, ashoo-**bleeft**.*
   Can I have some of that, please.

3. *Velkuh **hroont**uh?*
   Which vegetables?

4. ***Dayz**uh en **dee**.*
   These and those.

5. *Hoo-vayl **iss** dat?*
   How much is that?

Finding a seat, the lavatory

1. *Iss **dayz**uh plats **vray**?*
   Is this seat free?

2. ***Vaar** issduh vay-**say**?*
   Where are the toilets?

1. *Hooyuh **mor**khuh, (kannik/ **kunn**uh-vuh) ont-**bayt**uh?*
   Good morning, (can I/ can we) have breakfast, please?

2. *Vat **vilt**oo?*
   What would you like?

3. *Tay (koffee) **met** melk, ashoo-**bleeft**.*
   Tea (coffee) with milk, please.

4. *Makh-ik... ('n **mess**/ vat **broat**), ashoo-**bleeft**?*
   May I have... (a knife/ some bread) please?

een warme chocolademelk
*'n varmuh shokko-**laa**duh melk*
a Hot Chocolate

een koffie/thee
'n koffee/tay
a Coffee/Tea

brood/ broodjes/ toast
broat/ broat-yuss/ toast
Bread/ Rolls/ Toast

wat melk
vat melk
some Milk

warm/koud
varm/kowt
Hot/Cold

een ei
'n ay
an Egg

wat kaas/ham
vat kaass/ham
some Cheese/Ham

wat boter
vat boater
some Butter

wat jam
vat zhem
some Jam

1. *Ik vil 'n **taaf**el rayzer-**vay**ruh vor (van-**aav**ont/**zon**dakh).*
   I'd like to book a table for (this evening/Sunday).

2. *Vor hoo-vayl per-**soan**uh?*
   How many for?

3. *Vor (tvay) per-**soan**uh, vor akht uwr.*
   For (two), at 8 o'clock.

4. *Makh-ik oo **naam**, ashoo-**bleeft**?*
   What name, please?

phone p.53, days p.94, time p.55

1. *Hooyuh (**midd**akh/**aav**ont), hayft-oo 'n **taaf**el vor (tvay/dree) per-**soan**uh?*
   Good (afternoon/evening), have you a table for (two/three)?

2. *'N **oakh**en-blikyuh – hayft-oo khe**ray**zer-**vayrt**?*
   Just a moment – have you booked?

Ordering a meal

rood – rare
lichtgebakken – medium
doorgebakken – well done

4. Neemt u ook dessert?

5. Heeft het u gesmaakt?

1. Mag ik de menukaart, alsjeblieft?

2. Wat is de dagschotel?

3. Ik neem (het lamsvlees/ de steak). – Voor mij de vis.

6. Dat was erg lekker, dank u.

1. *Makh-ik duh muh-**nuw** kaart, ashoo-**bleeft**?*
   Could I have the menu, please?

2. ***Vat**-iss duh dakhs-**khoat**el?*
   What is today's special?

3. *Ik naym (hut **lamss**-vlayss/ duh stayk). - Vor **may** duh **viss**.*
   I'll have (the lamb/ the steak). - Fish for me.

4. ***Naym**too oak dess-**airt**?*
   Would you like dessert?

5. ***Hayft**-hut oo khuh-**smaakt**?*
   Did you like it?

6. *Dat vass **airkh lekk**er, dankoo.*
   That was very nice, thank you.

See also Queries and Problems, p.28

1. Ik ben vegetariër.

2. Heeft u ook vegetarische gerechten?

4. Doet u ook kinderporties?

3. (Zit er vlees) in dit gerecht?
   (Zitten er noten ...)

1. *Ik-ben vayhuh-taary-**air**.*
   I'm a vegetarian.

2. *Hayftoo oak vay-huh-**taar**issuh khuh-**rekht**uh?*
   Are there any vegetarian dishes?

3. *(Zitt er **vlayss**) indut khuh-**rekht**?*
   *(Zitten er **noat**uh...)*
   Has this dish got meat in?
   (Has it got nuts...)

4. *Dootoo oak **kind**er **por**seess?*
   Do you do children's portions?

5. Dit is niet wat ik bestelde. Ik vroeg ...

6. Kunt u dit wat langer bakken?

7. Dit is vies.

8. Dit ruikt/smaakt vies.

5. *Dit-iss **neet** vat-ik buh-**steld**uh.*
   Ik vrookh ...
   This isn't what I ordered.
   I asked for ...

6. *Kuntoo dit vat langer bakkuh?*
   Could you cook this a bit more, please?

7. *Dit-iss **veess**.*
   This is dirty.

8. *Dit **ruh**(oo)kt/ smaakt veess.*
   This smells/tastes bad.

9. Mag ik de rekening, alsjeblieft?

10. De rekening klopt niet.

9. *Makh-ik duh **ray**kening, ashoo-**bleeft**?*
   Could I have the bill, please?

10. *Duh **ray**kening **klopt** neet.*
    I think there's a mistake in the bill.

Ordering drinks

1. Wat wilt u drinken?
2. Een (glas/flesje) wijn, graag, en een flesje water.
3. Mag ik een glas water, alsjeblieft?

1. *Vat* viltoo drinkuh?
   What would you like to drink?

2. 'N (hlass/fleshuh) **vayn**, hraakh, en 'n fleshuh **vaa**ter.
   A (glass/bottle) of wine, please, and a bottle of mineral water.

3. Makh-ik 'n hlass **vaa**ter, ashoo-**bleeft**?
   Could I have a glass of water, please?

rode/witte wijn
roaduh/vittuh **vayn**
Red/White Wine

mineraalwater
minner-**aal** vaater
Mineral Water

spuitwater of plat?
spuh(oo)t-vaater
off **plat**?
Fizzy or Still?

Ice cream – *ijs, ijsjes*

2. Jawel, er is vanille, aardbeien en chocolade.
4. Groot of klein? Een of twee bolletjes?
5. Zo een.
1. Heeft u ook ijsjes?
3. Een chocoladeijsje, alsjeblieft.

zwarte bessen
svartuh bessuh
Blackcurrant

chocolade
shokko-**laad**uh
Chocolate

pistachio
pee-**stash**o
Pistachio

aardbeien
aardbayuh
Strawberry

vanille
van-**ee**yuh
Vanilla

1. *Hayft-oo oak* **ay**shuss?
   Have you any ice cream?

2. Ya-**vel**, er iss van-**ee**yuh, **aard**bayuh en shokko-**laad**uh.
   Yes, there's vanilla, strawberry or chocolate.

3. 'N shokko-**laad**uh **ay**shuh, ashoo-**bleeft**.
   A chocolate ice cream, please.

4. **Khroat** off **klayn**? Ayn off tvay **bollet**-yuss?
   Large or small? One scoop or two?

5. *Zo* ayn.
   One of those.

rundvlees,
runder-, osse-
beef

kalfsvlees,
kalfs-
veal

lamsvlees,
lams-
lamb

varkensvlees,
varkens- /ham
pork/ham

gevogelte/
wild
poultry /game

vis /schaal- en
schelpdieren
fish /seafood

vegetarisch   **een** - a
vegetarian
ik ben vegetariër *I'm ...*

Pronunciation: letters underlined should be stressed

AAL, aaltje	eel	**BALLETJES**	tiny meatballs
aardappel *-en*	potato/es	**banaan** *bananen*	banana/s
–puree	– mashed	**banketgebak**	pastries
aardbei *-en*	strawberry *-ries*	**basilicum**	basil
aardpeer	artichoke	**bataat** *bataten*	sweet potato/es
abrikozen	apricots	**bediening**	service
amandel *-en*	almond/s	**bedje: op een – van**	on a bed of
–gebak	– cake	**belegde broodjes**	filled rolls
ananas	pineapple	**belegen kaas**	mature cheese
andijvie	endive	**bereid met**	prepared with
anijs	aniseed	**bes** *bessen*	berry *berries*
ansjovis	anchovy	**beschuit**	rusk
appel, appeltje	apple	**op bestelling**	made to order
– beignets	– fritters	**biefstuk**	steak
– bol	– dumpling	**bieslook**	chives
– flap	– turnover	**(rode) biet** *-en*	beetroot
– gebak	– tart or cake	**bitterballen**	breaded meatballs
– moes	– puree	**bladerdeeg**	puff pastry
– pastel	– pie	**bleekselderij**	white celery
– sap	– juice	**blinde vinken**	stuffed, rolled veal
artisjok *-sjokken*	artichoke/s	**bloedworst**	black pudding
asperge, -punten	asparagus, – tips	**bloemkool**	cauliflower

boeren jongens	brandy: with raisins
boerenkool	curly kale
– met worst	– with smoked sausage
boerenomelet	omelette with diced vegetables, bacon
bonen, -saus	(broad) beans, – sauce
boontjes	runner beans
borrelhapjes	snacks for drinks
bos	wild
– bessen	bil/blueberries
– paddestoelen	wild mushrooms
– uitjes	small onions
– vruchtencompote	'wild' fruit compote
boter, -ham	butter; sandwich
... bout	leg, haunch
botersaus	butter, stock sauce
braadhaantje	spring chicken
braadworst	fried sausage
braambessen	blackberries
bronwater	spring water
broodje	roll
– 'gezond'	– salad
broodschoteltje	bread pudding with apples, currants
bruine bonen, -soep	brown beans, -soup
btw	VAT
CHAMPIGNONS	button mushrooms
chipolatapudding	pudding: biscuits, eggs, liqueur
chocolade	chocolate
– -ijs, -ijsje	– ice cream
– melk (warme-)	– drink (hot)
– saus	– sauce
chocomel	chocolate milk
citroen -en	lemon/s
– jenever	– gin
courgettes	courgettes/zucchini
DADELS	dates
dagschotel -s	today's special/s
dame blanche	vanilla ice cream, hot chocolate sauce
deeg	pastry
dille	dill
diverse (soorten)	different (kinds of)
doorbakken	well done
doornkreeften	crayfish
doperwten	green peas
dragon, –azijn	tarragon, – vinegar
dranken	drinks
drie kleuren	three colours
droog	dry
druiven	grape/s
duif	pigeon
ECHT/e	genuine, real
ei eieren	egg/s
–gerechten	– dishes
hard gekookt –	hard-boiled –
Russisch –	Russian –
spiegelei	fried –
zacht gekookt –	soft-boiled –
eiersalade	egg salad
eigengemaakt	home made
eend	duck
–elever	– liver
–enborst, -filet	– breast, fillet
erwten	peas
erwtensoep/ snert	thick pea soup, bacon, or sausage
eventueel	possibly
FARCE	stuffing
fazant	pheasant
fijn gehakt	finely chopped
flensjes	thin pancakes
forel forellen	trout
frambozen	raspberries
fricandeau	roast pork
frikadel	frankfurter sausage
frisdranken	sodas
friss/e	fresh
frites	chips/fries
GANS	goose
ganzenleverpastei	goose liver pâté
garnalen, -naaltjes	shrimps, prawns
garnituur	garnish

gebak	cake/s
gebakken	baked
– in de oven	– in the oven
gebraden	roasted
gefrituurd	deep-fried
gegarneerd	garnished
gegratineerd	breadcrumb topping maybe with cheese
gegrild	grilled
gehakt	minced meat
gehaktbal, -balletjes	meatball/s
geitenkaas	goat's cheese
gekookt	boiled
gemarineerd	marinated
gember	ginger
gemengde	mixed
– salade	– salad
gepaneerd	breaded
gepocheerd	poached
geraspt	grated
gerookt	smoked
geroosterd	grilled
gerst	semolina/couscous
geserveerd met	served with
gesmoord	braised
gesneden	sliced
gestoofd, met saus	stewed, with sauce
gevogelte	poultry
gevuld	stuffed
gewoon	normal, ordinary
goudbrasem	dory
graat	fish bone
griesmeel pudding	semolina
grietfilet	brill fillet
grill: van de –	from the grill
groene pepers	green peppers
groente -n	vegetable/s
–mix	mixed –

–soep	– soup
–taartje	– tart
HAAS	hare; tenderloin
hartige taart	savoury tart
Haagse bluf	whipped eggwhites, redcurrant sauce
half doorbakken	medium
ham (en eieren)	ham (and eggs)
hamblokjes	slices of ham
haring	herring
gerookte –	smoked –
nieuwe –	cured, fresh –
–salade	– salad
hazelnoot, -noten	hazelnut/s
hazenpeper	jugged hare
heilbot	halibut
heldere bouillon/soep	clear soup
hert	deer
heet, hete	hot
hete bliksem	potatoes, bacon, apple
herfstsalade	autumn salad
hochepot	meat, vegetable stew, fried sausage garnish
Hollandse: nieuwe	cured herring on toast
– saus	hollandaise sauce: butter, egg yolks
honing	honey
hoofdgerecht -en	main course/s
hoorntjes	pastry horns
hopjes	hard, coffee-flavoured sweets
houtsnip	woodcock
huiswijn	house wine
hutspot met klapstuk	beef & vegetable stew
huzarensalade	potato, apple, ham, gherkin, salad

IJS, ijsje	ice cream
–taart	– cake
ijsbergsla	iceberg lettuce
inbegrepen	included
ingewanden	tripe
inktvis	squid
JACHTSCHOTEL	meat stew, often with apple sauce
jagersaus	rich sauce: wine, herbs, mushrooms, shallots
jonge	early, young
– groenten	– vegetables

KAAS	cheese
–blokjes	– slices
–koekjes	– biscuits
–plankje	– board
–saus	– sauce
kabeljauw	cod
kalfs (-vlees)	veal
–borst	– breast
–haas	– tenderloin
–kotelet	– cutlet
–lapje	– escalope
–lever	– liver
–oester	– thin fillet
–rib	– chop
–schenkel	– knuckle
–zwezerik	– sweetbreads
kalkoen	turkey
kaneel	cinnamon
–beschuitjes	– rusks
kappers, kappertjes	capers
karamel, -saus	caramel, – sauce
karbonade -n	chop/s, cutlet/s
karnemelk	buttermilk
karper	carp
kastanjepuree	chestnut puree
kaviaar	cod's roe caviar
kerrie	curry
kersen	cherries
ketjapsaus	ketchup
kip	chicken
–filet	– fillet
** gebraden –**	– roast
–pensoep	– soup
klapstuk	thin flank (meat)
klein	small
knoflook; -saus	garlic; – sauce

knorhaan	red mullet
koekjes	biscuits, cookies
kokos|noot; -melk	coconut
komkommer	cucumber
konijn	rabbit
kool	cabbage
koolvis	whiting
kopstoot	beer with jenever chaser
korhoen	grouse
kort gebakken	rare
korstdeeg	puff pastry
kotelet -letten	chop/s, cutlet/s
koud	cold
krab	crab
krachtig	rich, full-bodied
kreeft, -je	crayfish
–saus	– sauce
–soep	– soup
krentenbol -bollen	bread rolls
krieken	cherries
krieltjes	Bantam hens
krokant	crispy
kroketten	croquettes, rissoles
kropsla	lettuce
kruiden , -boter	herbs, herb butter
kruidkoek	gingerbread
kruisbessen	gooseberries
kuiken	spring chicken
kummel	caraway
kwark	quark
kwartel	quail
LAMS- (vlees)	lamb
–bout	– leg
–curry	– curry
–kotelet	– chop

langoustinesaus	lobster sauce
lapje *-s*	escalope/s, steak/s
lauwwarm	lukewarm
lekker	delicious
lendenbiefstuk	beef loin
lente-ui, -uitjes	spring onion/s
lever	liver
likeur	liqueur
linzen	lentils
loempia	spring roll, vegetables, bean sprouts
look	leek/s
MAANZAAD broodje	poppyseed roll
maatjesharing	raw herring, onions
macaronischotel	macaroni, cheese, ham, tomato sauce
mager	skimmed, thin
maïskolven	corn on the cob
–koekjes	corn-cakes
makreel	mackerel
mandarijnen	tangerines
meelspijzen	pasta
meenemen	take-away
melange	mixture
meloen	melon
met	with
mierikswortel	horseradish
mooi/e	nice
mosselen	mussels
mosterd	mustard
–dressing	– dressing
–saus	– sauce
muskaatnoot	nutmeg
NAAR keuze	choice of
nagerechten	desserts
nieren, niertjes	kidneys
niet inbegrepen	excluded
noten, nootjesmix	nuts; assorted –

O.A.	also including
oesters	oysters
of	or
olie	olive oil
oliebollen	doughnuts
olijfbrood, -jes	olive bread, rolls
olijven	olives
omelet	omelette
boeren–	– vegetables, bacon
– met champignons	– mushroom
– met ham	– ham
– met kaas	– cheese
onbeperkt	unlimited
ongerezen brood	unleavened bread
ontbijtkoek	honey or ginger cake (for breakfast)
ook	also
op	on
opgediend	served
ossenhaas	fillet of beef
ossenstaartsoep	oxtail soup
ossetong	beef tongue
oude kaas	mature cheese
ouderwets	old fashioned
PADDENSTOEL *-en*	mushroom/s
paling	eel
gerookte –	– smoked
gesmoorde –	– stewed
gestoofde –	– stewed
– in 't groen	– green sauce, herbs
pannenkoeken	pancakes
pantser kreeft/ langoest	spiny lobster
paprika's	peppers
parelhoen	guinea fowl
passend	appropriate
pastei in korstdeeg	meat pie
pasteitje	filled pastry shell
patat, patates frites	chips/French fries
patrijs	partridge
peper	pepper
peer *peren*	pear/s
perzik *-en*	peach/es
peterselie	Parsley
peultjes	sugar peas
pijnboom pitten/pitjes	pine nuts
pikant	highly seasoned
pinda's	peanuts
pindakaas	peanut butter
pistache-nootjes	pistachio nuts

rolpens met rode kool	sliced, fried, minced meat & tripe roll, apple, red cabbage
rookvlees	smoked beef
rookworst	smoked sausage
romig/e	creamy
room	cream
−**boter**	creamy butter
−**kaas**	cream cheese
rosbief	roast beef
rozemarijn	rosemary
rozijnen, -zijntjes	raisins
runder-	beef
−**gehakt, -balletjes**	− meatballs
−**haas**	− tenderloin
−**lap**	− slice
−**rollade**	− roll, roasted
−**stoof**	− casserole
SALADE, - garnituur	salad, − garnish
salie	sage
sardientjes	small sardines
sateh	satay
saucijs, -ijsjes	sausage
saus *sauzen*	gravy, sauce/s
schaaldieren	seafood
schelp: in de −	in the shell
schelpdieren	shellfish
schelvis	haddock
schijf	slice
schol, scholletje	plaice, flounder
schotel *-s*	dish/es
seizoens-	seasonal
selder, selderij	celery
sesam broodje	sesame rolls
sesamzaadjes	" seeds
shoarma	kebab
sinaasappel *-s*	orange/s
−**appelsap**	− juice
sjalotten	shallots
sla	green salad
slagroom	whipped cream
slakken	snails
smeerkaas	cheese spread
snijbonen, -boontjes	sliced French beans
snoek	pike
snoekbaars	perch-pike
snoep	sweets
soep *-en*	soup/s
soesjes	choux pastries
soorten	sorts of

pittige saus/soep	spicy sauce/soup
pladijs	plaice
plak, plakje	slice
plakken spek	slice of bacon
pofaardappel	baking powder
poffertje *-s*	sugared fritter/s
pompelmoes	grapefruit
pompoensoep	pumpkin soup
poon, -filet	gurnard (fish), − fillet
potjesvlees	veal, chicken, rabbit in brawn
prei, -soep	leek, − soup
pruim *-en*	plum/s
gedroogde pruimen	prunes
RABARBER	rhubarb
radijsjes	radishes
rauwe of gekookt	raw or cooked
rauwkost	raw vegetables
ravigotesaus	sauce of hot or cold tarragon, chives, vinegar
recept	recipe
ree	venison
−**bout, -rug**	− haunch
reepjes kalkoen	turkey goujons
rijst	rice
−**ebrijpudding**	− pudding
−**timbaaltje**	− timbale
rivierkreeftjes	crayfish
riviervis	freshwater fish
rode poon	red mullet
roerei	scrambled eggs
roergebakken	stir-fried
rog	skate, ray
roggebrood	rye bread

specialiteit	speciality
speculaas	ginger/honey-flavoured biscuits
speenvarken	sucking pig
spek, spekjes	fat bacon
sperziebonen	green beans
spiegelei -eieren	fried egg/s
spiesje	on a skewer
spijs	food
spinazie	spinach
spruitjes	sprouts
stamppot	potato & vegetable hash, sausage/bacon
stoemp	mashed potato, meat/vegetable purée
stokbrood	French bread
stokjes	little pieces, sticks
stokvis	dried cod, rice, fried potatoes, mustard sauce
stoofappeltje-s	stewed apple/s
stoofpot	boiled beef
stoverij	beef & offal (liver, kidneys) stewed in beer, maybe bread with mustard
stroopwafels	waffles and syrup
stuk, stukjes	piece, small pieces
suiker	sugar
TAART, taartje	tart, individual –
tarbot	turbot
taugé	Moroccan style cereal/couscous
tijm	thyme
toast, toastje	toast
toeslag	supplement
toetje	sweet
tomaten	tomato

gevulde –	– stuffed
–sap	– juice
–saus	– sauce
–soep	– soup
tong	tongue; sole (fish)
tonijn	tuna
–salade	– salad with potato, vegetables
truffel	truffle
tuinbonen	broad beans
tuinkers	cress
tussenrib	rib steak
UIEN: -ringen	onion: rings
–soep	– soup
uitjes	small onions
uitsmijter	ham or cheese, fried eggs on bread
VAN	of
varkens- (vlees)	pork
–haas, -je	– fillet
–karbonade	– chop
–kotelet	– chop, cutlet
vegetarisch	vegetarian
venkel,-bootje,-knol	fennel
verschillende	selection of
vers/e	fresh
vetarm/e	low fat
vijgen	figs
vis	fish
–fileetje	small fillet
–gerechten	– dishes
–pot	– stew
–rollade	– roullade
vissersoep	– soup
vla	custard
Vlaamse bloedworst	black pudding with apples
Vl. hazepeper	jugged hare, onions, plums
Vl. karbonade	beef & onions stewed in beer
Vl. kool	cabbage, apples, gooseberry jelly
vlees: -schotel	meat: dish
–waren	pork meats
voor twee personen	for two
voorgerecht -en	appetizer/s
vossebessen	cranberries
vruchten: -sap	fruit: juice

−sla	− salad
vulling	filling
WAFEL -s	waffle/s
waterkers	watercress
waterzooi	chicken, vegetable white wine stew
− met vis	fish soup
wentelteefjes	pan-baked bread
wijnsaus	wine sauce
wijting	whiting
wild	game
−bouillon	− soup, bouillon
−ragout	− ragout
−saus	− sauce
−stoof	− stew
wilde zwijn	wild boar
wit/witte	white
witlof	endive, chicory
witte bonen	haricot beans
worst -en	sausage/s
wortelen, -teltjes	carrots
ZACHT	tender, soft
zalm	salmon
−eitjes	− roe
−filet	− fillet
−foreleitjes	− trout roe
gerookte −	− smoked
−mousse	− mousse
zee	sea
−tong doria	poached sole, cucumber, rice, tarragon sauce
−vis	− fish
−vruchten	−food
zilveruitjes	spring onions
zoals 't hoort	'as it used to be'
zoet/e	sweet
zoetzure	sweet & sour sauce
zonder	without
zout/e	salt, salty
zoutjes	salty biscuits (snacks)
zuur, zure	sour, marinated
zuurkool	sauerkraut
zwarte bessen	blackcurrants

INDONESISCHE GERECHTEN
Indonesian dishes

Ajam	chicken
Atjar	pickles
Babi pangang	grilled pork, sweet & sour sauce
Bami	fried noodles, pork/ chicken, vegetables
Daging	beef
Gado gado	vegetables, peanut sauce
Goreng	fried
Ikan	fish
Katjang	peanut
Kroepoek	shrimp crackers
Loempia	egg rolls
Nasi Goreng	fried rice, meat, chicken, prawns, ham, egg strips
Nasi Rames	one-plate *rijsttafel*
Pedis	hot and spicy
Pisang	banana
Rijsttafel	set banquet of spicy dishes with plain rice
Sambal	hot, chilli-based sauce
Satesaus	peanut sauce for kebabs
Seroendeng	spicy fried shredded coconut
Tauge	bean shoots

ENGLISH-DUTCH

cold	koud
fat; greasy	vet
gluten-free	gluten-vrij
hot, spicy	pikant
nuts	noten
salt, salty	zout
too	te
I'm vegetarian	ik ben vegetariër
wheat	de tarwe
with/without	met/zonder

Is hier een ... in de buurt?
Iss heer 'n ... induh buwrt?
Is there a ... near here?

OPER   GESLOTEN
oaper   *khuh-sloatuh*
Open   Closed

Hours: normally 9am to 6pm, though many shops close all or part of Monday. Some stay open until 9pm on *Koopavond* (shopping night) – usually Thursday.

How to ask: Often you don't need the actual name, just point and say:

Mag ik dat daar?   or   **Wat van die**
*makh-ik **dat** dar?*   *vat-van **dee***
Can I have that one, please?   Some of that, please

* * *

Heeft u ook (appels)?
*hayft-oo oak (**appels**)?*
Have you any (apples)?

Wat (appels), alsjeblieft
*vat (**appels**), ashoo-**bleeft***
Some (apples), please

Hoeveel kost dat?
*hoo-vayl **kost** dat?*
How much is that?

Hoeveel?
*hoo-**vayl**?*
How much/many?

Een kilo tomaten
*'n keelo to-**maa**tuh*
A kilo of (tomatoes)

Een, twee
ayn, tvay
One, two

Deze, die
***day**zuh, dee*
This one, that one

Een stuk ...
'n stuk ...
A piece (of) ...

Een halve kilo
*'n **hal**vuh keelo*
1/2 kilo

Honderd gram
hondert khram
100 g

Groot, klein, half
khroat, klayn, halff
Big, small, half

Wat (meer/minder)
*vat (mayr/**min**-der)*
A bit (more/less)

Verder nog iets?
***vair**der nokh-**eets**?*
Anything else?

Dat is goed
*dat-iss **khoot***
That's fine

Per stuk
Each

Ik kijk maar rond
*ik **kayk** maar ront*
I'm just looking

Het spijt me...
*hut **spayt**muh ...*
I'm sorry...

Aanbieding
Special offer

N.B. When handing someone something, say **alsjeblieft** *(ashoo-bleeft)*, meaning *Here you are*. The conversation pattern at the baker's can be used in all shops.

2. *'N (khroat/klayn) broat, hraakh.* **Zoan** *broat.*
   A (large/small) loaf, please. One like that.
3. *En* **nokh** *vat broat-yuss -* **tvay**, *hraakh.*
   And some rolls - two, please.

1. *Dakh!* **Zekht**-*oo hut* **maar.**
   Good morning, can I help you?

1. *Ashoo-***bleeft**, **vair**der nokh-**eets***?*
   Here you are. Would you like anything else?

2. **Nay**, *dankoo, dat-iss* **alluss.** *Hoo-vayl* **iss** *dat?*
   No, thanks, that's all. How much is that?

3. *Dat-***iss** *dan ...* **saa**muh.
   That's ... altogether.

4. *Ashoo-***bleeft**.
   Here you are.

5. *Dankoo.* **Tot** *seenss.*
   Thank you. Goodbye.

Butcher – *de slager* – *slaakher*   *het vlees* - meat
(in *English* order; Dutch order in *Menu Guide*)

Graag (wat) ...
Hraakh (vat) ...
(some) ... please

rundvlees
runt-vlayss
Roast Beef

kip
kip
Chicken

een eend
'n aynt
a Duck

(kalfs)lapjes
(kalffs) lap-yuss
Escalopes

wild
vilt
Game

lam
lam
Lamb

varkensvlees
varkens-vlayss
Pork

konijn
kon-ayn
Rabbit

biefstuk
beefstook
Steak

ingewanden
inkhuh-vanduh
Tripe

kalkoen
kal-koon
Turkey

karbonaden	**lever**	**gehakt**	**worst**	**kalfsvlees**
kaarbo-naaduh	*layver*	*khuh-hakt*	*vorst*	*kalffs-vlayss*
Chops	Liver	Mince	Sausages	Veal

Delicatessen   *Fijne en bereide vleeswaren*

bloedworst
blootvorst
Black Pudding

ham
ham
Ham

paté
pat-ay
Pâté

pizza
peetsa
Pizza

een quiche
'n keesh
a Quiche

salami
sa-laamee
Salami

kabeljauw	**schelvis**	**makreel**	**schol**	**een forel**
*kabbel-**yow***	*s'**hel**viss*	*mak-**rayl***	*s'holl*	*'n fo-**rell***
Cod	Haddock	Mackerel	Plaice	a Trout

krab	**haring**	**mosselen**	**garnalen**	**tonijn**
krap	*haaring*	***moss**eluh*	*khar-**naa**luh*	*ton-**ayn***
Crab	Herring	Mussels	Prawns/Shrimps	Tuna

schar	**bokking**	**oesters**	**zalm**	**wijting**
s'haar	*bokking*	***oost**erss*	*zal(uh)m*	*vayting*
Dab/Flounder	Kipper	Oysters	Salmon	Whiting

paling	**kreeft**	**snoek**	**tong**	
paaling	*krayft*	*snook*	*tong*	
Eel	Lobster	Pike	Sole	

Vis – Zeevruchten
fish – seafood

Vegetables – *groenten* – *hroontuh*
(in *English* order; Dutch order in *Menu Guide*)

artisjokken
arti-shokkuh
Artichokes

knoflook
k(uh)nofloak
Garlic

sla
slaa
Lettuce

uien
uh(oo)-uh
Onions

asperges
ass-pairzhuss
Asparagus

prei, look
pray, loak
Leeks

champignons
shampeen-yonss
Mushrooms

erwten
airvtuh
Peas

aubergines
oabair-zheenuss
Aubergines/Eggplants

een avocado
'n avvo-kaado
an Avocado

boontjes
boant-yuss
Runner Beans

rode biet
roaduh beet
Beetroot

groene/witte kool
hroonuh/vittuh koal
green/white Cabbage

wortelen
vorteluh
Carrots

bloemkool
bloomkoal
a Cauliflower

selder
selder
Celery

witlof
vitloff
Chicory

Graag (wat) ...
Hraakh (vat) ...
(some) ... please

een **tas**
'n tass
a Bag

courgettes
kuwr-zhet
Courgettes/Zucchini

een (rode/groene) peper
'n (roaduh/hroonuh) payper
a (red/green) Pepper

radijsjes
rad-ayshuss
Radishes

maïs
'mice'
Sweetcorn

een komkommer
'n kom-kommer
a Cucumber

aardappelen
aard appeluh
Potatoes

spinazie
spee-naazee
Spinach

tomaten
tom-aatuh
Tomatoes

Fruit – *vrucht* – *frowt*

appels
appels
Apples

abrikozen
*abbree-**koa**zuh*
Apricots

bananen
*ban-**aanuh***
Bananas

bosbessen
***boss** bessuh*
Bil-/Blueberries

braambessen
***braam** bessuh*
Blackberries

kersen/krieken
kairsuh/kreekuh
Cherries

aalbessen
***aal** bessuh*
Currants

vijgen
vay-khuh
Figs

kruisbessen
***kruh**(oo)ss bessuh*
Gooseberries

een pompelmoes
*'n **pompel**-muss*
a Grapefruit

druiven
***druh**(oo)-vuh*
Grapes

een citroen
*'n see-**troon***
a Lemon

een meloen
*'n **mull**oon*
a Melon

noten
noatuh
Nuts

sinaasappelen
***see**naas-**app**eluh*
Oranges

een ananas
*'n **anna**-nass*
a Pineapple

pruimen
***pruh**(oo)-muh*
Plums

frambozen
*fram-**boa**zuh*
Raspberries

rabarber
*rab-**arber***
Rhubarb

aardbeien
***aard**bayuh*
Strawberries

een watermeloen
*'n **vaat**er **mull**oon*
a Water Melon

een perzik
*'n **pair**zik*
a Peach

peren
payruh
Pears

bier
beer
Beer

Graag (wat) ...
Hraakh (vat) ...
(some) ... please

Heeft u ...?
Hayft-oo ...?
Have you any ...?

koekjes
kook-yuss
Biscuits/Cookies

pasta
pasta
Pasta

boter
boater
Butter

rijst
rayst
Rice

ontbijtgranen
*ont-**bayt** hraanuh*
Cereal

zeeppoeder
***zayp** pooder*
Soap Powder

kaas
kaass
Cheese

suiker
***suh**(oo)-ker*
Sugar

koffie
koffee
Coffee

thee
tay
Tea

eieren
***ay**eruh*
Eggs

WC papier
*vay-**say** pap-**eer***
Toilet Paper

fruitsap
frowt sap
Fruit Juice

afwasproduct
af**vass pro-**dukt
Washing-up Liquid

honing
hoaning
Honey

water
vaater
Water

jam
zhem
Jam

yoghurt
***yokh**urt*
Yogurt

margarine
*markha-**ree**nuh*
Margarine

zout
zowt
Salt

(magere/halfvolle) melk
*(**maa**kheruh/**halff** volluh) melk*
(skimmed/semi-skimmed) Milk

peper
payper
Pepper

olie
oalee
Oil

mosterd
***moss**tert*
Mustard

Where can I get ...? *Waar vind ik ...?* *vaar vint-ik...?*
Can I have ...? *Mag ik ...?* *makh-ik...?*

Books — Stationery — Newspapers — Films

een boek (over)
'n book (over)
a Book (about)

een (Engels-Nederlands)
*'n **eng**-elss **nay**der-lants*
a (Dutch-English)
woordenboek
vorduh-book
Dictionary

een (Engelse) krant
*'n (**eng**-elser) krant*
an (English) Newspaper

een filmrolletje (voor **dia's**)
*'n film **roll**ut-yuh (vor dee-ass)*
a (slide) Film

een potlood
*'n **pot**-loat*
a Pencil

een balpen
*'n **bal**-pen*
a Ballpoint Pen

een landkaart (over)
*'n **lant**-kaart (over)*
a Map (of)

een stratenplan
*'n **straa**tuh-plan*
a Street Map

Cigarettes etc.

Household articles

een prentbriefkaart
*'n **prent**breef-kaart*
a Postcard

sigaretten
*sikha-**rett**uh*
some Cigarettes

met filter
met filter
with Filter

een aansteker
*'n **aan**staykuh*
a Lighter

een kurkentrekker
*'n **kur**kuh trekker*
a Corkscrew

een postzegel
*'n **posst**-zaykhel*
a Stamp

een batterij
*'n batter-**ay***
a Battery

lucifers
loossy-fairss
some Matches

een postzegel

een zaklantaarn
*'n **zak**-lantaarn*
a Torch/Flashlight

een flessenopener
*'n **fless**uh op**ener**
a Bottle Opener

een naald
'n naalt
a Needle

garen
khaaruh
some Thread

een schaar
'n s'haar
some Scissors

een blikopener
*'n **blik** opener*
a Tin/Can Opener

een touwtje/ touw
'n towt-yuh/ tow
some String/Rope

> Heeft u iets tegen ... ?
> *Hayft-oo eets **tay**khen ...?*
> Have you anything for ...?

een schaafwondje
*'n s'**haaf** vont-yuh*
a Graze

insectenbeten
*in-**sek**tuh-baytuh*
Insect Bites

zonnebrand
***zonn**uh-brant*
Sunburn

hoofdpijn
***hoaft**-payn*
a Headache

constipatie
*konsti-**paa**see*
Constipation

hoesten
khoostuh
a Cough

diaree
*dee-a **ray***
Diarrhoea

oorpijn
***or**-payn*
Earache

hooikoorts
***hoy**-korts*
Hay Fever

reisziekte
***rayss**-zeektuh*
Sea Sickness

keelpijn
***kayl**-payn*
a Sore Throat

maagpijn
***maakh**-payn*
Stomach Ache

Toiletries etc.

> Mag ik (wat) ...
> *Makh-ik (vat)* ...
> Could I have (some) ...

ontsmettingsmiddel
ont-smettingss middel
Antiseptic Cream

aspirine
aspee-reenuh
Aspirin

babyvoeding
baby fooding
Baby Food

een verband
'n ver-bant
a Bandage

een kam
'n kam
a Comb

condomen
kon-doamuh
Condoms

watten
vattuh
Cottonwool

insectenverwerend middel
in-sektuh ver-vayrent middel
Insect Repellant

crème voor de billetjes
krem vorduh billet-yuss
Nappy Cream

luiers
luh(oo)-erss
Nappies/Diapers

deodorant
dayodor-ant
a Deodorant

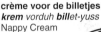

pleisters
playsterss
Plasters/Band-Aid

een scheermes
'n s'hayrmess
a Razor

papieren zakdoekjes
pap-eeruh zakdook-yuss
Paper Handkerchiefs

zeep
zayp
Soap

scheercrème
s'hayr-krem
Shaving Cream

maandverband (tampons)
maant ver-bant (tam-ponss)
Sanitary Napkins/Towels (Tampons)

shampoo
shampoa
Shampoo

tandpasta
tan-pasta
Toothpaste

zonnebril
zonnuh-brill
Sunglasses

zonnecrème
zonnuh-krem
Suntan Cream

een tandenborstel
'n tanduh-borstel
a Toothbrush

een hoed
'n hoot
a Hat

een muts
'n muts
a Woolly Hat

een hemd/blouse (T-shirt)
'n hemt/bloozuh (tee shirt)
a Shirt/Blouse (T-shirt)

een rok
'n rok
a Skirt

een herenslip/damesslip
*'n **hay**ruh-/**daa**muh-slip*
Men's/Women's Briefs

nylons
*nay*lonss
some Tights

een jurk
'n yurk
a Dress

een zwempak/zwembroek
*'n **zvem**pak/**zvem**brook*
a Swimming Costume/Trunks

een broek
'n brook
some Trousers

een paar sokken
*'n par **sokk**uh*
some Socks

een trui/pullover
*'n **truh**(oo)/pull-**ov**er*
a Sweater

een jas/regenjas
*'n yass/ **ray**khuh-yass*
a Coat/Raincoat

een jeans/spijkerbroek
*'n jeanss/**spay**kerbrook*
some Jeans

een paar schoenen
*'n par s'**hoon**uh*
a pair of Shoes

een sjaal
'n shaal
a Scarf

een short
'n short
some Shorts

handschoenen
hans-khoonuh
some Gloves

een broeksriem
*'n **brooks**reem*
a Belt

een zakdoek
*'n **zak**dook*
a Handkerchief

Buying clothes

1. *Kannik oo **helpuh?***
   Can I help you?

2. *Ik **zook** 'n **truh**(oo).*
   I'd like a sweater.

3. *Velkuh **maat** hayft-oo?*
   What size do you take?

4. *Ik **hep** maat **fayr**tukh.*
   I take size 40.

5. ***Hayft**-oo **day**zuh oak in (**bl-ow**)?*
   Have you got this in (blue)?

1. *Makh-ik dit **ayvuh aan**-passuh?*
   Can I try it on?

2. ***Day**zuh maat iss per-**fekt**. Hut zit lekker.*
   This size is fine.
   It fits very well.

3. *Hut past **neet**.*
   It doesn't fit.

4. *Hut-iss (tuh **khroat**/ tuh **klayn**).*
   It's (too big/ too small).

5. *Hut-iss tuh **duwr**.*
   It's too dear.

1. *Ik naym **day**zuh. Vat **kost** dee?*
   I'll take this. How much is it?

2. *Oo kunt anduh **kass**a buh-**taa**luh.*
   Please pay at the cash desk.

3. *Kannik buh-**taa**luh met (kred-**it** kaart/*
   ***doll**aarss/ **rayss** shecks)?*
   Can I pay with (a credit card/
   dollars/ traveller's cheques)?

4. *Ashoo-**bleeft**.*
   Here you are.

5. *Dankoo.*
   Thank you.

Exchanges/complaints

1. Kunt u dit wisselen?

2. Ik wil een klacht indienen.

3. Kunt u me de aankoopsom terugbetalen?

4. Hier is het bonnetje.

1. ***Kun**too dit **viss**eluh?*
   Can you change this?

2. *Ik vil 'n **klakht in**deenuh.*
   I want to make a complaint.

3. ***Kun**too-muh duh **aan**koopsom te**rukh**-buhtaaluh?*
   Can you give me a refund?

4. ***Heer** iss hut **bonn**et-yuh.*
   Here's the receipt.

wat geld
*vat **khelt***
some money

kleingeld
***klayn**-khelt*
change

kontant betalen
*kon-**tant** buh-**taal**uh*
to pay cash

1. Waar vind ik een geldautomaat/bank)?

2. Ginds, op het plein.

1. ***Vaar** vintik 'n (**khelt** owtoh-**maat**/ bank)?*
   Where will I find a (cash dispenser/ bank)?

2. ***Khints**, opput **playn**.*
   Over there, in the square.

To change money look for *Change* sign

2. Mag ik uw (paspoort/ identiteitskaart), alsjeblieft?

3. Kunt u hier even tekenen.

4. U kunt uw geld bij de kassier afhalen.

1. Mag ik (dollars/ reischeques) wisselen?

1. *Makh-ik **doll**aarss/ **rayss** shecks **viss**eluh?*
   Can I change some dollars/traveller's cheques?

2. *Makh-ik oo (**pass**port/ eedenty-**tayts**kaart), ashoo-**bleeft**?*
   Could I have your (passport/identity card), please?

3. *Kuntoo **heer** ayvuh **tay**kenuh.*
   Please sign here.

4. *Oo kunt oo **khelt** bayduh kass-**eer af**haaluh.*
   You can collect the money from the cashier.

Waar is het postkantoor?
*Vaar iss-hut **posst** kan-**tor**?*
Where is the post office, please?

1. Verkoopt u postzegels?

2. Voor (Groot-Brittanië/ de Verenigde Staten).

1. *Ver-**koapt** oo **posst** zaygulss?*
   Do you sell stamps?

2. *Vor (khroat bree-**tan**yuh/ duh **vray**nikh-duh staatuh).*
   To (Great Britain/ the USA, please).

Stamps are also sold at newsagents.

Postboxes are red. **Overseas** mail: use slot marked *Overige*.

Festivals and public holidays – *Publieke feestdagen*

NL	New Year's Day	January 1	*Nieuwjaarsdag*	B
NL	Good Friday		*Goede Vrijdag*	
NL	Easter Monday		*Paasmaandag*	B
NL	Queen's Birthday	April 30	*Koninginnedag*	
	Labour Day	May 1	*Dag van de Arbeid*	B
NL	Liberation Day	May 5	*Bevrijdingsdag*	
NL	Ascension Day	40 days after Easter	*Hemelvaartsdag*	B
NL	Whit Monday	7th Mon. after Easter	*Pinkstermaandag*	B
	National Day	July 21	*Nationale Feestdag*	B
	Assumption	August 15	*Maria Hemelvaart*	B
	All Saints' Day	November 1	*Allerheiligen*	B
	Armistice Day	November 11	*Wapenstilstandsdag*	B
NL	St Nicholas's Day	December 5	*Sinterklaas*	
NL	Christmas Day	December 25	*Kerstmis*	B
NL		December 26		
	New Year's Eve	December 31	*Oudejaaravond*	

NB In Belgium, if any of these fall on a Sunday, the next day is a holiday.

Telephone – *de telefoon*

> Is hier een telefoon
> in de buurt?

Iss *heer 'n tayluh-**foan** induh* **buwrt**?
Is there a phone near here?

> Mag ik de telefoon
> gebruiken?

*Makh-ik duh tayluh-**foan**
khuh-**bruh**(oo)kuh?*
Could I use your phone,
please?

> Mag ik een
> telefoonkaart?

> Hoeveel eenheden?

*Makh-ik 'n tayluh-**foan kaart**?*
A phone card, please.

*Hoo-vayl **ayn**-hayduh?*
How many units?

> 1. Hallo.
> 2. Dit is ...
> 3. Kan ik met ...
>   spreken, alsjeblieft?
> 4. Een ogenblikje.

1. *Hallo.*
   Hello.

2. *Dit-iss ...*
   This is ...

3. *Kannik met ... **spray**kuh,
   ashoo-**bleeft**?*
   Can I speak to ... please?

4. *'N **oa**khuh-blikyuh.*
   Please hold.

Emergency numbers (no card required)
Netherlands 112
Belgium Fire/Accidents 100
       Police 101

Instructions

Most phones only take credit cards (with
a chip) or phone cards *telefoonkaarten,*
sold at post offices, tourist offices or
station kiosks.

Instructions are usually given in English.
Lift handset and press *English* button.
Welkom. Steek kaart in.
'Welcome. Insert card'.

Information/Reverse-charge/Collect calls

Inland directory enquiries	0900-8008
International " "	0900-8418

Names are listed alphabetically,
disregarding the prefixes *de, van, van der.*

Inland reverse-charge/ collect calls	0800-0101
International reverse-charge/ collect calls	0800-0410

Numbers (p.131) are given in groups,
eg 112 34 56 (honderd twaalf, drieëndertig,
zesenvijftig).

Ringing home

Dial 00, the country code, and then your
local code minus the first 0. Similarly, when
ringing Holland or Belgium from abroad,
omit the first 0 of the local code.

Australia	00	61
Eire	00	353
New Zealand	00	64
UK	00	44
US & Canada	00	1
Belgium		32
Netherlands		31

A	aa		N	en
B	bay		O	oh
C	say		P	pay
D	day		Q	kuw
E	ay		R	airr
F	ef		S	ess
G	khay		T	tay
H	haa		U	uw
I	ee		V	vay
J	yay		W	v(w)ay
K	kaa		X	iks
L	el		Y	ay/ypsilon
M	en		Z	zet

Hoe spel je dat?
*Hoo **spell**-yuh dat?*
How do you spell that?

Taxi – *een taxi*

Tip: 10% anticipated

1. Waar vind ik een taxi?
2. Kunt u een taxi bellen alsjeblieft?
3. Naar ... (de luchthaven/ het station), alsjeblieft.
4. Wat zal dat kosten?
5. Mag ik een bonnetje?

1. ***Vaar** vintik 'n **tax**i?*
   Where will I find a taxi*?

2. *Kuntoo 'n **taxi** belluh, ashoo-**bleeft**?*
   Can you call a taxi, please?

3. *Naar ... (duh **lukht**-haaver/ hut stass-**yon**), ashoo-**bleeft**.*
   To ... (the airport/ the station), please.

4. ***Vat** zaldat **kost**uh?*
   How much will it cost?

5. *Makh-ik 'n **bonnet**-yuh?*
   Could I have a receipt, please?

You will usually need to ring, or to find a taxi rank: een taxistandplaats
   *'n taxi **stant**-plaats*

Treintaxi

Many Dutch stations (not in Amsterdam, Rotterdam or The Hague) operate a taxi-sharing service (maximum wait 10 minutes), taking you anywhere in the town for a flat rate per person. You can buy *een Treintaxi-biljet* (undated ticket) from the station ticket office or machine, or (dearer) from the driver.

If no taxi is waiting, press the yellow knob for the *Taxi-centrale*. You can also phone them to order a taxi to the station.

Wheelchairs are carried if users can get in and out of taxis without assistance.

Time

Hoe laat is het?
Hoo laat iss-hut?
What's the time?

NB half past = half to
Dutch-speakers think of the half hour
as halfway to the next hour,
e.g. half past three = half vier (4)
(if in doubt, use figures: drie uur dertig).

Het is ... een uur
Hut-iss ... ayn uwr
It's ... one o'clock

tien over drie
teen over dree
ten past three

vijf over twee
vayf over tvay
five past two

kwart over vier
k(uh)vart over feer
quarter past four

tien voor half zes
teen vor halff zess
twenty past five

half acht
halff akht
half past seven

vijf voor half zeven
vayf vor halff zayvuh
twenty-five past six

vijf over half acht
vayf over halff akht
twenty-five to eight

tien over half negen
teen over halff naykhuh
twenty to nine

tien voor elf
teen vor elf
ten to eleven

kwart voor tien
k(uh)vart vor teen
quarter to ten

vijf voor twaalf
vayf vor tvaalf
five to twelve

Full-scale business negotiations are beyond the scope of this book. This section will enable you to negotiate the switchboard or reception desk, make appointments and leave messages. Some product and financial terms are also included.

May I speak to –?

1. Mag ik spreken met (de Heer/Mevrouw ...)?
3. Het is het nummer ...
2. Weet u (zijn/haar) toestelnummer?
4. Blijf aan de lijn alsjeblieft.
5. De lijn is bezet.
6. Wilt u even wachten?

1. *Makh-ik **spray**kuh met (duh-**hayr**/muv-**row** ..)?*
   May I speak to (Mr/Ms ...) please?

2. ***Vay**too (zayn/haar) **toos**tel-nummer?*
   Do you know (his/her) extension?

3. ***Hut** iss hut **num**mer ...*
   It's ...

4. ***Blayf** anduh **layn**, ashoo-**bleeft**.*
   Please hold.

5. *Duh **layn** iss buh-**zet**.*
   It's engaged.

6. ***Vil**too ayvuh **vakht**uh?*
   Do you want to hold?

1. Ik wil spreken met... de directeur (de verantwoordelijke voor de: uitvoer/verkoop).
2. Weet u (zijn/haar) naam?
4. Kunt u me (zijn/haar) nummer geven, alsjeblieft?
3. De persoon die u wenst te spreken is (de Heer/Mevrouw ...) in ons kantoor in ...

1. *Ik vil **spray**kuh met...*
   *duh deerek-**tuwr***
   *(duh ver-**ant**vordelukkuh vorduh:*
   ***uh**(oo)t-vor/ ver-**koap**).*
   I'd like to speak to... the manager (the person in charge of: exports/sales).

2. ***Vay**too (zayn/haar) **naam**?*
   What's (his/her) name?

3. *Duh per-**soan** dee oo venst-tuh **spray**kuh iss (duh-**hayr**/muv-**row** ...) in onss kan-**tor** in ...*
   You need to speak to (Mr/Ms ...) at our office in ...

4. ***Kun**too-muh (zayn/haar) **num**mer **khay**vuh, ashoo-**bleeft**?*
   Could you give me (his/her) number, please?

Who's calling?

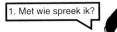

> 3. Kunt u dat even spellen?
> 4. En de naam van uw firma?
>
> 2. Dit is ...
>
> 1. Met wie spreek ik?

1. *Met **vee sprayk**-ik?*
   Who's calling?

2. *Dit **iss** ...*
   This is ...

3. ***Kun**too dat ayvuh **spell**uh?*
   Can you spell that, please?

4. *Enduh **naam** vannoo **feer**ma?*
   And the name of your company?

They're not available

> 1. (Hij/zij) is er nu niet.
> 2. Het spijt me, (de Heer/Mevrouw ...) is in vergadering.
>
> 3. Wanneer is (hij/zij) vrij?
> 4. Ik bel later terug.

1. *(Hay/zay) isser nuw **neet**.*
   (He/she) is not in at present.

2. *Hut **spayt**muh, (duh-**hayr**/muv-**row** ...) iss in ver-**khaa**dering.*
   I'm sorry, (Mr/Ms ...) is in a meeting.

3. *Van-**ayr** iss (hay/zay) **vray**?*
   When do you expect (him/her) to be free?

4. *Ik bel **laa**ter ter-**ukh**.*
   I'll call back later.

Leaving a message

> 1. Kan ik een boodschap achterlaten?
> 2. Kunt u (hem/haar) vragen of (hij/zij) even terugbelt?
>
> 3. Wat is het telefoonnummer? Het nummer van (zijn/haar) GSM?
>
> 4. Het nummer is ...

> 5. Dank u wel.
>
> 6. Tot uw dienst.

1. *Kannik 'n **boads**-khap **akht**er-laatuh?*
   Can I leave a message, please?

2. *Kuntoo (hem/haar) **vraak**huh off (hay/zay) ayvuh ter-**ukh**belt?*
   Could you ask (him/her) if (he/she) can ring me back?

3. ***Vat** iss hut tayluh-**foan** nummer? Hut **nummer** van (zayn/har) khay ess **em**?*
   What's the phone number? The number of (his/her) mobile phone?

4. *Hut **nummer** iss ...*
   The number is ... *

5. *Dankoo **vel**.*
   Thank you very much.

6. *Tottoo **deenst**.*
   Not at all. *Nos. p.131

1. *Hooyuh (**mor**khuh/**midd**akh). Kannik oo **hel**puh?*
   Good (morning/afternoon). Can I help you?

2. *Ik hep 'n **af**-spraak met (mun-**nayr**/muv-**row** ...) om **elf** uwr.*
   I have an appointment with (Mr/Ms ...) at 11 o'clock.

3. ***Zay**ker, (mun-**nayr**/muv-**row**). Makh-ik oo **naam**, ashoo-**bleeft**?*
   Certainly, (sir/madam). Could I have your name, please?

4. *Enduh **naam** vanoo **feer**ma?*
   And the name of your company?

5. *Ik ver-**tay**khuh-**vor**dukh ...*
   I represent ...

6. ***Heer** iss mayn **kaart**-yuh.*
   Here's my card.

(days p.94, time p.55, nos. p.131)

Making an appointment

1. *Ik vil **hraakh** 'n **af**-spraak maakuh met (duh-**hayr**/muv-**row** ...)*
   I'd like to make an appointment to see (Mr/Ms ...)

2. *... bay **vor**kuwr (**smor**khuns/ **smidd**akhs).*
   ... preferably (in the morning/ in the afternoon).

3. *Ik ben **vray** (**mor**khuh/ op **maan**dakh/ op feer **may**).*
   I am free (tomorrow/ on Monday/ on 4 May).

4. *(Hay/zay) kanoo ont-**fang**-uh (dinss-dakh elf), om **dree** uwr.*
   (He/she) can see you on (Tuesday 11), at 3 o'clock.

5. *S'**hikt**oo **dat**?*
   Is that convenient?

6. *Tot **seenss** dan.*
   I look forward to meeting you.

7. *Ik **hoap** datvuh **saa**muh **zaa**kuh kunnuh-**doon**.*
   I hope we can do business together.

Finding the office – *het kantoor*

1. *Naym-duh **lift** naarduh ... ver-**deep**ing.*
   Take the lift to the ... floor.

2. *(Hay/zay) **kom**ter **net** an.*
   (He/she) is just coming.

1st	eerste	*ayrstuh*
2nd	tweede	*tvayduh*
3rd	derde	*dairduh*
4th	vierde	*veerduh*
5th	vijfde	*vayfduh*
6th	zesde	*zesduh*

1. *Prettikh mettoo **kenn**istuh **maak**uh.*
   I'm delighted to meet you.

2. ***Kann**ik-oo mun koll-**ay**guh (mun-**nayr**/muv-**row** ...) **vor**stelluh.*
   May I introduce my colleague, (Mr/Ms ...).

3. ***Tot** seenss.*
   I look forward to meeting you again.

4. ***Dank**oo, en tot **seenss**.*
   Thank you, and see you again.

Fax, photocopying, phoning - and thanks

1. Heeft u mijn (brief/ fax/ email) ontvangen?
   *Hayft-oo mayn (breef/ fax/ email) ont-**fang**-uh?*
   Have you received my (letter/ fax/ email)?

2. Kan ik een fax versturen, alsjeblieft?
   *Kannik 'n **fax** ver-**stuw**ruh, ashoo-**bleeft**?*
   Could I send a fax, please?

3. Wat is uw fax nummer?
   *Vat-iss oo **fax** nummer?*
   What's your fax number?

4. Wat is uw email adres?
   *Vat-iss oo **ee**mail add**ress**?*
   What's your email address?

5. Ik wil een brief laten typen.
   *Ik vil 'n **breef** laatuh **ty**puh.*
   I need to have a letter* typed.

6. Kunt u dit voor me photocopiëren?
   *Kuntoo dit **vor**muh fotokop-**yair**uh?*
   Could you photocopy this for me?

7. Mag ik uw telefoon gebruiken?
   *Makh-ik oo tayluh**foan** khuh-**bruh**(oo)kuh?*
   Could I use your phone, please?

8. Het hoeft niet per se (vandaag/nu). (Morgen/laater) is OK.
   *Hut **hoaft** neet per-**say** (van**daakh**/nuw). (**Mor**khuh/**laa**ter) iss OK.*
   It doesn't need to be done (today/now). (Tomorrow/later) will be fine.

9. Hartelijk dank. Ik ben u erg dankbaar.
   ***Har**tuh-luk dank. Ik ben oo **airkh** dankbar.*
   Thank you for your help. I'm extremely grateful.

*Addresses: Dhr. for men, Mevr. for women.
In Belgium the surname often precedes the first name.

Office equipment

de computer
duh computer
the Computer

computer software/programma
*computer **soft**ware/pro**gram**ma*
Computer Software/Programme

een diskette
*'n dis-**kett**uh*
a Disk

een projector
*'n proy-**ek**tor*
an Overhead Projector

Ik wil graag wat informatie over ...
*Ik vil **hraakh** vat infor-**maa**see over ...*
    I'd like some information about ...

Kunt u me een lijst van uw producten met prijzen toesturen ...
***Kun**too-muh 'n **layst** vanuw pro-**dukt**uh **met** prayzuh too-**stuw**ruh ...*
    Could you send me a list of your products and a price list ...

... voor machines met een productiecapaciteit van 200 kg per uur.
*... vor ma-**shee**nuss met 'n pro-**duk**see kapasi-**tayt** van 200 **kee**logram per **uw**r.*
... for machines capable of processing 200 kg/hour.

een vertegenwoordiger
*'n vur-**tay**khuh-**vor**dukher*
a Representative

een tak
'n tak
a Branch

een verdeler
*'n ver-**day**ler*
a Distributor

het hoofdbureau
*hut **hooft** buw-**ro***
the Head Office

publiciteitsmateriaal
*puwblisi-**tayts** matree-**aal***
Publicity Material

een dochterbedrijf
*'n **dokht**er bud-**rayf***
a Subsidiary

The product

de assemblage
*duh assum-**blaa**zhuh*
the Assembly

een groep (producten)
*'n khroop (pro-**dukt**uh)*
a Batch of (Production)

een component
*'n **kom**po-nent*
a Component

een product
*'n pro-**dukt***
a Product

een productenprogramma
*'n pro-**dukt**uh pro-**gramm**a*
a Product range

een nieuwe lijn
*'n **new**-uh layn*
a New Line

de grondstoffen
*duh **khront**-stoffuh*
the Raw Materials

de eindproducten
*duh **aynt**pro-**dukt**uh*
the Finished Products

de productielijn
*duh pro-**duk**see layn*
the Production Line

naar keuze
of your Choice

een bestellingsnota
an Order Form

een bestelling plaatsen
to Place an Order

een contract
a Contract

een contract toekennen
to Award a Contract

de gevraagde
leveringsdatum
the Delivery Date
Requested

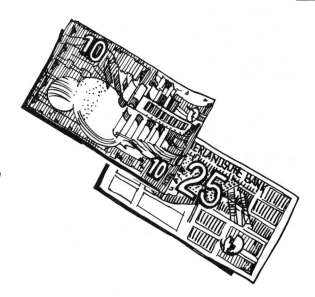

Finance

We staan een korting toe van ... procent.
*Vuh-**staan** 'n korting **too** van ... pro-**sent**.*
    We would allow a discount of 30%.

Onze jaaromzet bedraagt ... per jaar.
*Onzuh **yaar**-omzet buh-**draakht** ... per **yaar**.*
    We have a turnover of (3 million) a year.

op voorhand
in Advance

de prijs is inclusief/exclusief
the Price is Inclusive/Exclusive

een rekening
a Bank Account

een bankkaart
a Banker's Card

een cheque
a Cheque

de commissie
the Commission

de kosten
the Costs

in de lokale munteenheid
in local Currency

een schatting
an Estimate

factureren
to Invoice

een (pro-forma) factuur
a (pro forma) Invoice

een prijsopgave
a Quotation

de interest
the Rate of Interest

een rekeningsuittreksel
a Statement of Account

een kwitantie
a Receipt

netto prijs
before Tax

het totaal
the Total

een transfer maken
to make a Transfer

BTW
VAT

schriftelijk
in Writing

noord
noort
North

zuid
zuh(oo)t
South

west
vest
West

oost
oast
East

het strand
hut strant
the Beach

de brug
duh brookh
the Bridge

de gracht
duh khrakht
the Canal
(narrow, in towns)

het kanaal
*hut kuh-**naal***
the Canal (wide)

**het
kasteel/paleis**
*hut ka-**stayl**/
pal-**ayss***
the Castle/Palace

de kathedraal
*duh kattay-**draal***
the Cathedral

de kerk
duh kairk
the Church

de bioscoop
*duh bee-o-**skoap***
the Cinema

de heuvel/berg
*duh **hur**vel/bairkh*
the Hill

het eiland/meer
*hut **ay**lant/mayr*
the Island/Lake

de markt/~plaats
*duh markt/~**plaats***
the Market/~place

het museum
*hut muw-**zay**um*
the Museum

het park
hut parrk
the Park

het politiebureau
*hut po**lit**see buw-**ro***
the Police Station

de tunnel
*duh **tunn**el*
the Tunnel

de vallei
*duh val-**ay***
the Valley

de windmolen
*duh **vint**moaluh*
the Windmill

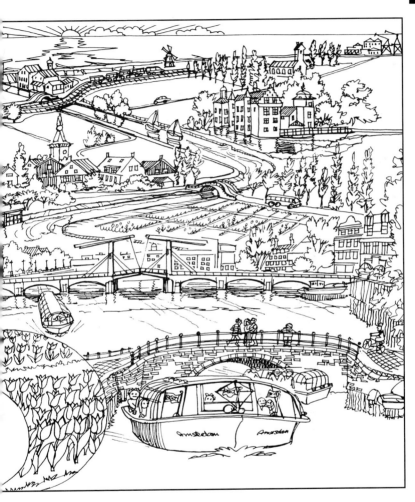

het theater
hut tay-aater
the Theatre

het stadscentrum
hut stat-sentrum
the Town Centre

het bos/woud
hut boss/vow-t
the Wood

Waar is ...?
vaar iss ...?
Where is ...?

Hoe ga ik naar ...?
hoo khaa ik naar ...?
How do I get to ...?

de VVV
duh vay vay vay

het bureau voor toerisme
hut buw-ro vor too-reezmuh
the Tourist Office (NL/B)

1. *Per-**don**, vaar **iss** ...?*
   Excuse me, where is ...?

2. ***Stayk** duh straat over en naym duh (**ayr**stuh) straat **rekhts**.*
   Cross the road and take the (first) right.

3. *Iss **dit** duh **vekh** naar ...?*
   Is this the way to ...?

4. ***Naym** duh vekh naar ...*
   Take the road to ...

5. *Hoo **vair** iss-hut?*
   How far is it?

Directions/locations

de W.C./ het toilet	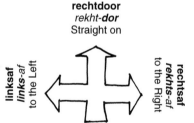 W.C.	**rechtdoor** *rekht-**dor*** Straight on
*vay-**say**/ twa-**let*** the Lavatory	*Dames* Ladies *Heren* Gentlemen	
Vrij Vacant	*Bezet* Engaged	

linksaf *links-af* to the Left

rechtsaf *rekhts-af* to the Right

achter, voor *akhter, vor* Behind, in Front

op de hoek *op**duh** hook* on the Corner

het kruispunt *hut **kruh**(oo)ss punt* the Crossroads

tot aan *tot **aan*** as Far as

hier, daar *heer, daar* Here, There

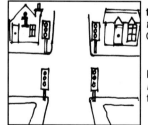

tegenover *taykhun-**over*** Opposite

het rondpunt *hut **ront**-punt* the Roundabout

naast *naast* Next to

de verkeerslichten *duh ver-**kayrss** likhtuh* the Traffic Lights

> **Prettige reis!**
> *prettikhuh rayss*
> Have a good trip!

de auto
duh ow-toh
the Car

de fiets, de motorfiets
duh feets, duh mo-tor feets
the Bicycle, the Motorcycle

ik loop
ik loap
I walk

Speed limits:
Belgium 50km in towns, 90 other roads, 120 motorways (31, 56, 75mph)
Netherlands 50, 80, 120km (31, 50, 75mph)

On the open road

Priority: traffic from **right** has priority
unless stated otherwise.
NB If road is shared with trams and/or
bicycles, they have priority.

Your   right   of   way

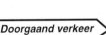

Doorgaand verkeer

Through traffic

No longer your
right of way

Give way

Andere richtingen

Other destinations

One-way street

*U rijdt
te snel*

Slow down

Look out for
bicycles

*Uitgezonderd
(brom)fietsen*

Except (mopeds)
bicycles

Centrum

Town centre

uitgezonderd...

Except ...

*Marken
volg 2*

For *Marken*
follow 2

*Ontsteek
uw lichten*

Use headlights

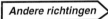

Expressway/motorway *de autosnelweg - ow-toh snelvekh*

afrit 26
600 m

Exit 26

UIT

Exit

file/s

Traffic jam

filevrij

Road clear

een parkeerplaats - a car park

niet parkeren (vanaf)

No parking (from)

alleen voor...

Only for...

betaald parkeren

Parking fee

bezoekers

Visitors (to)

geldt niet voor parkeermeters en automaten

Does not apply to meters/machines

uitsluitend...

Except/only...

... in de vakken

... in marked spaces

... na afspraak

... by prior arrangement

parkeerschijf verplicht

Disc zone

Park + Ride

... toegestaan

... permitted

vergunning-houders

Permit holders

Day/time

t/m to... inclusive

van, vanaf, v.a. ... tot...
from...   to...

ma maandag Mon.
di dinsdag Tues.
wo woensdag Wed.
do donderdag Thurs.
vr vrijdag Fri.
za zaterdag Sat.
zo zondag Sun.

op koopavond/en
on late shopping night/s

tarief – per h
Tariff – per hour

Parkeergarage
Multi-storey car park

Westzijde VOL VRIJ
Full   Spaces

Meters

*Maak erst uw keuze
met de GELE knop*

*KEUZE 1 – / 60 min
Minimale inworp Fl.-*

*KEUZE 2
DAGKAART – per dag
Gepast betalen!*

Geld teruggave

een parkeermeter/automaat

Select option using
YELLOW button

OPTION 1 – / 60 mins.
Minimum payment

OPTION 2
All-day ticket – per day
Insert exact amount.

Refund

The bicycle – *de fiets* – feets

Holland has many cycle paths, often with their own traffic lights. If using the same carriageway as motor vehicles, bicycles (and trams) have priority. Most bike shops hire out bikes, as do main stations - though they must be returned to the same station. You will need an extra ticket for the bike and must put it on the train yourself.

Fietsers		**Fietspad**
Cyclists	Obligatory cycle path	Optional cycle path

Breakdown/emergency (phone p.53, repairs p.72)

Look for yellow emergency phones (all are numbered).
Kilometer posts are every 100m.

1. Mijn auto is defect.
2. Kunt u me helpen, alsjeblieft?
3. Mag ik uw telefoon gebruiken?
4. Waar is de dichtstbijzijnde garage?
5. Waar is de auto nu?
6. Welk merk is de wagen?

Instructions

1. Place vehicle as far from road as possible.
2. Switch on warning lights.
3. Place warning triangle 30m behind vehicle.
4. All occupants of car should stand on verge.
5. Get in and out of car by right-hand door.

1. *Mayn **ow**-toh iss dee-**fekt**.*
   My car has broken down.
2. ***Kun**too-muh **help**uh, ashoo-**bleeft**?*
   Can you help me, please?
3. *Makh-ik oo tayluh-**foan** khuh-**bruh**(oo)kuh?*
   Could I use your phone, please?
4. *Vaar issduh **dikhts**bay-zaynduh khuh-**raa**zhuh?*
   Where is the nearest garage?
5. *Vaar issduh **ow**-toh **nuw**?*
   Where is the car now?
6. *Velk **mairk** issduh **vaa**khuh?*
   What make is the car?

De ... werkt niet.
*duh ... **vairkt** neet*
The ... isn't working.

De motor start niet.
*duh motor **start** neet*
The engine won't start.

Ik heb een ... nodig.
*ik **hep** 'n ... noa-dukh*
I need a ...

De motor slaat af.
*duh motor slaat **af***
The engine is stalling.

1. de **batterij**   *een* - a
   *duh batter-**ay***
   the Battery

2. de **remmen**
   duh remmuh
   the Brakes

3. het **remlicht**
   *hut **rem**likht*
   the Brake Light

4. de **remblokken**
   *duh **rem**-blokkuh*
   the Brake Blocks

5. de **gloeilamp**
   *duh **khloo**-ee lamp*
   the Bulb

6. de **kabel**
   duh kaabul
   the Cable

7. de **carburateur**
   *duh karbuw-**raa**tor*
   the Carburettor

8. de **ketting**
   duh ketting
   the Chain

9. de **versnellingspook**
   *duh ver-**snell**ingss poak*
   the Clutch

10. het **electrische systeem**
    *hut ay**lek**trissuh si**staym***
    the Electrical System

11. de **motor**
    *duh **mo**tor*
    the Engine

12. de **uitlaat**
    *duh **uh**(oo)t-laat*
    the Exhaust

13. de **V-snaar**
    *duh **vay** snaar*
    the Fan Belt

14. het **lucht-/olie-filter**
    hut lukht/oalee filter
    the Air/Oil Filter

15. de **zekering**
    *duh **zay**kering*
    the Fuse

16. de **pakking**
    duh pakking
    the Gasket

17. de **versnelling**
    *duh ver-**snell**ing*
    the Gears (bicycle)

18. de **versnellingsbak**
    *duh ver-**snell**ingss-bak*
    the Gearbox

19. het **stuur**
    hut stuwr
    the Handlebars

20. de **koplamp**
    *duh **kop**-lamp*
    the Headlight

21. de **contactsleutel**
    *duh kon-**takt** slurtel*
    the Ignition Key

22. de **binnenband**
    *duh **binn**uh-bant*
    the Inner Tube

23. de **olie-/water-tank lekt**
    duh oalee/vaater tank lekt
    the Oil/Water Tank Leaks

24. de **lamp**
    duh lamp
    the Light

25. het **bagagerek**
    *hut buh-**gaa**zhuh-rek*
    the Luggage Carrier

26. de **bagageriem**
    *duh buh-**gaa**zhuh-reem*
    the Luggage Strap

27. de **moer**
    duh moor
    the Nut

28. de **onderbreker punten**
    *duh **on**terbraykuh **pun**tuh*
    the Points

29. de **pomp**
    duh pomp
    the Pump

30. de **reparatiekit**
    *duh raypa-**raa**see kit*
    the Puncture Kit

31. de **radiator**
    *duh raddy-**aa**tor*
    the Radiator

32. de **schroef**
    duh s'khroof
    the Screw

33. de **schroevedraaier**
    *duh s'**khroo**vuh **dry**-er*
    the Screwdriver

34. de **schokdemper**
    *duh s'**khok** demper*
    the Shock Absorber

35. de **geluidsdemper**
    *duh khull-**uh**(oo)ts demper*
    the Silencer

36. de **(moer)sleutel**
    duh slurtel
    the Spanner

37. de **kaars**, de **bougie**
    *duh kaarss, boo-**zhee***
    the Spark/Glow Plug

38. de **spaken**
    duh spaakuh
    the Spokes

39. de **band**
    duh bant
    the Tyre

40. de **banddruk**
    *duh ban-**drook***
    the Tyre Pressure

41. de **klep**
    duh klep
    the Valve

42. het **wiel**
    hut veel
    the Wheel

43. de **voorruit**
    *duh **vor**-uh(oo)t*
    the Windscreen/-shield

44. de **ruitewissers**
    *duh **ruh**(oo)tuh-visserss*
    the Windscreen Wipers

Auto/Fietsen te huur
Car/Cycle hire

sneeuwkettingen
***snay**(oo) **kett**inguh*
Snow Chains

ik heb een lekke band
*ik hep 'n lekkuh **bant***
I've got a Puncture/Flat

Is hier een benzinestation in de buurt?
Iss heer 'n ben-zeenuh stass-yon induh buwrt?
Is there a filling station near here?

1. (Diesel). Voltanken, alsjeblieft.
2. Kunt u (het oliepeil/de banddruk) even nakijken?

benzine	**diesel**
ben-zeenuh	*diesel*
Petrol/Gas	Diesel
autogas	**antivries**
ow-toh khass	*anti-vreess*
LPG	Antifreeze

lucht	**olie**	**water**
lukht	*oalee*	*vaater*
Air	Oil	Water

1. *(Deezul).* **Vol**-*tankuh, ashoo-***bleeft**.
   (Diesel.) Fill it up, please.
2. *Kuntoo (hut **oalee**-payl/ duh ban-**drook**) ayvuh naa-**kay**kuh?*
   Can you check (the oil/ the tyre pressure), please?

Repairs

1. Wat is er aan de hand?
2. De ... werkt niet.
3. Kunt u het repareren?
4. Hoe lang gaat dat duren?
5. Wat gaat dat kosten?
6. Dank u wel.

1. ***Vat** isser anduh **hant**?*
   What's the matter?
2. *Duh ... **vairkt** neet.*
   The ... isn't working.
3. *Kuntoo hut raypa-**ray**ruh?*
   Can you mend it?

4. ***Hoo**-lang khaat-dat **duwr**uh?*
   How long will it take?
5. ***Vat** khaat-dat **kost**uh?*
   What do I owe you?
6. *Dankoo **vell**.*
   Thank you very much.

regelen - to adjust   *nakijken* - to check   *gebogen* - bent   *het zit vast* - it's stuck

1a. *Dakh (mun-**nayr**/muv-**row**). Ik hep 'n **ow**-toh khurrayzuh-**vayrt**. Mayn **naam** iss ...*
Hello (sir/madam). I have booked a car. My name is ...

1b. *Dakh (mun-**nayr**/muv-**row**). Ik vil 'n **ow**-toh **huwruh**.*
Hello (sir/madam). I'd like to hire a car.

2. *Vatvor **ow**-toh: klayn, **may**dee-um, khroat?*
What sort of car: small, medium, large?

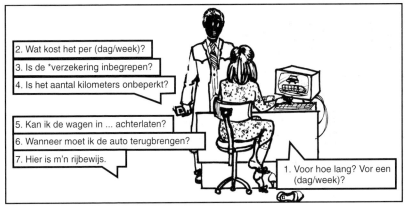

1. *Vor **hoo**-lang? Vor 'n (dakh/vayk)?*
For how long? For a (day/week)?

2. *Vat **kost** hut per (dakh/vayk)?*
How much is it per (day/week)?

3. *Issduh ver-**zay**kering **in**buh-khraypuh?*
Is *insurance included?

4. *Iss-hut aantal **keel**omayterss onbuh**perkt**?*
Is it unlimited mileage?

5. *Kannik duh **vaa**khen in ... **akh**ter-laatuh?*
Can I leave the car in ...?

6. *Van-**ayr moot**ik duh **ow**-toh ter**ukh**-brenguh?*
When do I have to return the car by?

7. ***Heer** iss mun **ray**buh-vayss.*
Here is my driving licence.

*omnium - comprehensive

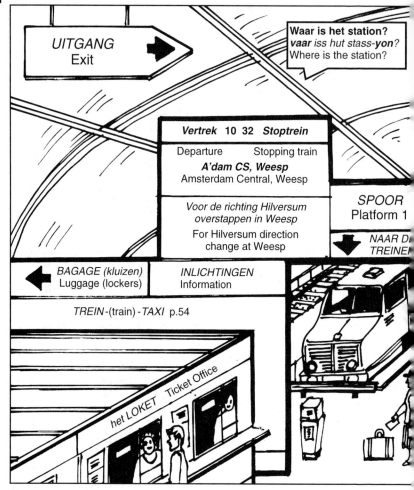

UITGANG
Exit

Waar is het station?
vaar iss hut stass-yon?
Where is the station?

Vertrek 10 32 Stoptrein

Departure   Stopping train
A'dam CS, Weesp
Amsterdam Central, Weesp

Voor de richting Hilversum overstappen in Weesp
For Hilversum direction change at Weesp

SPOOR
Platform 1

NAAR D⟮
TREINE⟮

BAGAGE (kluizen)
Luggage (lockers)

INLICHTINGEN
Information

TREIN-(train)-*TAXI* p.54

het LOKET Ticket Office

Ticket machines

1. Find 4-figure destination code
2. *Toets code in* – Enter code

3. *Maak keuze* – Select option
   2e klas - 2nd class 1e klas - 1st
   ----
   alleen vandaag geldig
   valid today only

   zonder datum
   undated; must be stamped
   on (first) day of travel)

(3. cont.) *enkele reis*   *retour*
   single   return
   5-retour kaart – 5-return card
   (must be stamped on day of travel)

   weekend retour – weekend return
   valid for outward journey on Friday
   from 19.00 and on Saturday
   ----

4. *Betaal* – Pay
   Bij vergissing indrukken
   Made a mistake? Press here

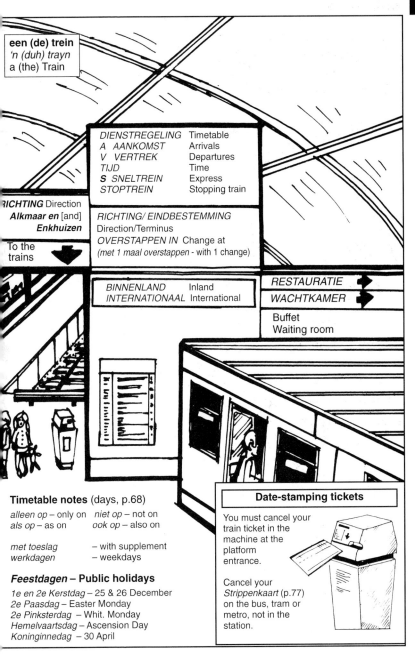

een (de) trein
'n (duh) trayn
a (the) Train

DIENSTREGELING	Timetable
A AANKOMST	Arrivals
V VERTREK	Departures
TIJD	Time
S SNELTREIN	Express
STOPTREIN	Stopping train

RICHTING Direction
Alkmaar en [and]
Enkhuizen

To the trains

RICHTING/ EINDBESTEMMING
Direction/Terminus
OVERSTAPPEN IN Change at
(met 1 maal overstappen - with 1 change)

| BINNENLAND | Inland |
| INTERNATIONAAL | International |

RESTAURATIE

WACHTKAMER

Buffet
Waiting room

Timetable notes (days, p.68)

alleen op – only on *niet op* – not on
als op – as on *ook op* – also on

met toeslag – with supplement
werkdagen – weekdays

Feestdagen – Public holidays

1e en 2e Kerstdag – 25 & 26 December
2e Paasdag – Easter Monday
2e Pinksterdag – Whit. Monday
Hemelvaartsdag – Ascension Day
Koninginnedag – 30 April

Date-stamping tickets

You must cancel your train ticket in the machine at the platform entrance.

Cancel your *Strippenkaart* (p.77) on the bus, tram or metro, not in the station.

1. Een enkele reis naar ... alsjeblieft.
2. Wat kost dat?
3. Kan ik een (zitplaats/slaapplaats) boeken?
4. Wanneer vertrekt de trein naar ...?
5. Moet ik overstappen?

Waar wilt u naar toe?
vaar viltoo naar-too?
Where do you want to go?

Ik wil naar ...
ik vil naar ...
I want to go to ...

Enkele reis (naar)
enkeluh rayss (naar)
Single/One way (to)

Heen en terug (naar)
hayn en terukh (naar)
Return/Round trip (to)

Rokers of niet-rokers?
roakerss off neet roakerss?
Smoker or Non-smoker?

1. *'N enkeluh rayss naar ... ashoo-bleeft.*
   A single to ... please.
2. *Vat kost dat?*
   How much is it?
3. *Kannik 'n (zitplaats/slaap-plaats) bookuh?*
   Can I book a (seat/couchette)?
4. *Van-ayr ver-trekt duh trayn naar ...?*
   When does the train to ... go?
5. *Mootik over-stappuh?*
   Moet ik overstappen?

de volgende/laatste
duh volgun-duh/ laatstuh
the Next/Last

3. Spoor drie.
1. Ik heb m'n trein gemist.
2. Op welk spoor staat de trein voor ...?
4. Is dit de trein voor ...?

1. *Ik hep mun trayn khum-ist.*
   I've missed my train.
2. *Op velk spor staat duh trayn vor ...?*
   Which is the platform for ...?
3. *Spor dree.*
   Platform three.
4. *Iss dit duh trayn vor ...?*
   Does this train go to ...?

Bus/tram – *de bus/tram* – *buwss/tram*

1. Hoe kom ik bij ...?
2. Wanneer vertrekt de bus naar ...?
3. Waar vertrekt de bus naar ...?
4. Hoe vaak gaat de bus?

de bushalte
*duh **buwss** haltuh*
the Bus Stop

ingang In
uitgang Out
drukken Press

koop uw kaartjes hier
Tickets sold here

1. *Hoo **komm**ik bay ...?*
   How do I get to ...?

2. *Van-**ayr** ver-**trekt** duh **buwss** naar ...?*
   When does the bus to ... go?

3. ***Vaar** ver-**trekt** duh buwss naar ...?*
   Where does the bus to ... go from?

4. *Hoo-**vaak** khaat duh **buwss**?*
   How often does the bus go?

Een strippenkaart, alsjeblieft -
twee (drie, acht) strippen.
*'n **stripp**enkaart, ashoo-**bleeft** -
tvay (dree, akht) strippuh.*
A strip ticket, please - 2, (3, 8) strips.

Strippenkaarten: sold at
stations, post offices, many
shops and valid on trams, buses,
metro throughout Holland.
Cancel in the machine when you
get on: 1 strip, plus 1 for each
zone required. Changing allowed
within the hour. Several people
may use one card - cancel same
number of strips for each.

1. Gaat deze bus naar ... (het station)?
2. Is dit ... (het station)?
3. Kunt u me zeggen waar ik moet afstappen?

1. *Khaat **day**zuh **buwss** naar ... (hut stass-**yon**)?*
   Does this bus go to ... (the station)?

2. ***Iss** dit ... (hut stass-**yon**)?*
   Is this ... (the station)?

3. ***Kun**too-muh **zay**khuh vaar ik moot **af**stappuh?*
   Can you tell me when to get off?

Holland uses *Strippenkaarten*
Belgium has a flat fare

1. **Ayn** *kaart-yuh, ashoo-**bleeft**.*
   One, please.
2. *Hoo **kommik** bay ...?*
   How do I get to ...?
3. **Naym** *layn ... naar ...*
   Take line ... to ...
4. *Moot-ik **ov**erstappuh?*
   Do I have to change?

(speech bubble)
1. Een kaartje, alsjeblieft.
2. Hoe kom ik bij ...?
3. Neem lijn ... naar ...
4. Moet ik overstappen?

Boat/ferry – *de boot/de ferry* – boat/ferry

1. Waar vandaan vertrekt de boot naar ...? Wanneer?
2. Hoe lang duurt de reis?

3. Kan ik een (slaapzetel/ cabine) reserveren?

1. **Vaar** *van-**daan** ver-**trekt** duh boat naar ...? Van-**ayr**?*
   Where does the boat to ... go from? When?
2. *Hoo-**lang** duwrt duh **rayss**?*
   How long does it take?

3. *Kannik 'n (**slaap**-zaytel/ kab-**ee**nuh) rayzer-**vay**ruh?*
   Can I book a (reclining chair/cabin)?

Bakboord – Port
bakbort

het **kanaal**
*hut kuh-**naal***
the Canal (wide)

de **haven**
duh haavuh
the Harbour

de **zwemgordel**
*duh zvem-**khord**ul*
the Lifebelt

de **buitenboordmotor**
***buh**(oo)ten-bort motor*
the Outboard Motor

Stuurboord – Starboard
stuwrbort

de **sluis**
*duh **sluh**(oo)ss*
the Lock

de **jachthaven**
*duh **yakht** haavuh*
the Marina

het **zwemvest**
*hut zvem-**vest***
the Lifejacket

Help!
help!
Help!

Gevaar!
*khuh-**vaar**!*
Danger!

1. Waar is het kantoor van de havenmester?
2. Waar vind ik scheepsonderdelen?
3. Waar kan ik (water, olie, diesel, ijsblokken) vinden?
4. Waar vind ik een machinist?
5. Wanneer gaat de sluis (open/dicht)?

1. *Vaar iss hut kan-**tor** vanduh **haav**uh-mayster?*
   Where is the harbour master's office?

2. *Vaar vintik **skhayps on**derdayluh?*
   Where is the ships' chandlery?

3. *Vaar kannik (vaater, oalee, deezul, **ayss**-blokkuh) vinduh?*
   Where can I get some (water, oil, diesel, blocks of ice)?

4. *Vaar vintik 'n mashee-**nist**?*
   Where will I find a (marine) engineer?

5. *Van-**ayr** khaat duh **sluh**(oo)ss (oapuh/dikht)?*
   When does the lock (open/close)?

Waar vind ik een weersvoorspelling?
*Vaar vintik 'n **vayrs**-vorspelling?*
Where will I get a weather forecast?

---

de **douanebeambte**
*doo-**aan**uh buh-**am**tuh*
the Customs Officer

het **registratiekantoor**
*raykhi-**straa**see kan-**tor***
the, Port of Registry

stormwaarschuwing
*storm vaars-**khuw**ving*
Gale warning

hoge/lage druk
hoakhuh/laakhuh druk
High/Low pressure

de **stroming**
duh stroaming
the Current

de zee
duh zay
the Sea

ruwe (kalme) zee
*ruwvuh (**kal**muh) zay*
Rough (Calm) sea

ebbe en vloed
ebbuh en vloot
Low and High Tide

toenemende/	**afnemende/**	**middelmatige ...**	**wind**	het **tij**
too-naymenduh/	*af-naymenduh/*	*middel-**maat**ukhuh*	*vint*	*hut tay*
increasing/	decreasing/	moderate ...	Wind	the Tide

Hoe kom ik bij de luchthaven?
***Hoo** kommik bayduh **lukht**-haavuh?*
How do I get to the airport?

aankomst / vertrek
Arrivals/Departures

binnenlandse / buitenlandse
Domestic/International

Instappen bij uitgang nummer ...
*Instappuh bay **uh**(oo)t-khang nummer ...*
Boarding will take place at gate number ...

Laatste oproep voor passagiers voor
vlucht ... naar ...
***Laat**stuh **op**roop vor passa-**kheerss** vor
vlukht ... naar ...*
Last call for passengers on
flight ... to ...

1. Wanneer is de volgende vlucht naar ...?
3. Wanneer moet ik inchecken?
4. Wat is het vluchtnummer?
5. Is het een directe vlucht?

1. *Van-**ayr** issduh **vol**gun-duh vlukht naar ...?*
   When is the next flight to ...?

2. *Om **teen** over **nay**khuh.*
   At ten past nine.

3. *Van-**ayr** moot-ik **in**checkuh?*
   What time is check in?

4. *Vat-iss hut **vlukht**-nummer?*
   What is the flight number?

5. *Iss-hut 'n dee-**rek**tuh vlukht?*
   Is it a direct flight?

Problems, reservations

1. Ik heb m'n vliegtuig gemist.
2. Mijn bagage is niet aangekomen.
3. Ik wil mijn boeking veranderen
4. Mag ik een ticket voor New York voor maandag 4 (mei), alsjeblieft.

1. *Ik **hep** mun **vleekh**-tukh khuh-**mist**.*
   I've missed my plane.

2. *Mayn bag-**aazh**uh iss neet **an**khuh-koamuh.*
   My luggage hasn't arrived.

3. *Ik vil mayn **booking** ver-**ander**uh.*
   I'd like to change my reservation, please.

4. *Makh-ik 'n tick-**ett** voor **New** York vor **maan**dakh veer (may), ashoo-**bleeft**.*
   Could I have a ticket to New York, for Monday 4 (May), please.

Accidents and illness

Ziekenhuis

Hospital

Emergency (no phonecard needed)
Netherlands (all services) 112
Belgium

Fire	*Brandweer*	100
Accidents	*Ongevallen*	100
Politie	*Police*	101

1. Help!
2. Vlug! Bel een ziekenwagen!
3. Waar is het ziekenhuis?

Minor ailments: p.46

1. *Help!*
   Help!
2. *Vlookh! **Bell** 'n **zee**kuh-vaakhuh!*
   Quick! Call an ambulance!

3. ***Vaar** iss hut **zee**kuh-huh(oo)ss?*
   Where is the hospital?

Calling the doctor/making an appointment

1. Wat is er aan de hand?
2. Ik heb (een dokter/een ziekenwagen) nodig.
3. Kan ik een afspraak maken?
4. Wanneer? Het is dringend.

een dokter/arts
a doctor

Eerste Hulp-post
First Aid post

de polikliniek
Out-patients' Department

de verzekering
the insurance

een ziekenwagen/ambulance
an ambulance

1. *Vat **iss**-er aanduh **hant**?*
   What's the matter?
2. *Ik **hep** ('n **dok**ter/'n **zee**kuh-**vaa**khuh) noadukh.*
   I need (a doctor/an ambulance).

3. *Kannik 'n **af**-spraak **maa**kuh?*
   Can I make an appointment?
4. *Van-**ayr**? Hut iss **dring**-ent.*
   When? It's urgent.

(Parts of the body p.85)

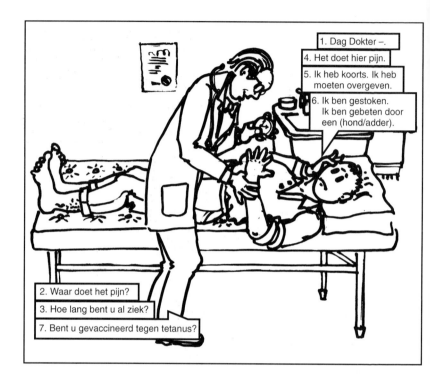

1. *Dakh dokter –.*
   Hello, doctor –.

2. ***Vaar** doot-hut **payn**?*
   Where does it hurt?

3. ***Hoo**-lang bent-oo al **zeek**?*
   How long have you been ill?

4. *Hut doot **heer** payn.*
   It hurts here.

5. *Ik hep **koorts**. Ik hep mootuh **over**-khayvuh.*
   I have a temperature. I've been vomiting.

6. *Ik ben khuh-**stoa**kuh. Ik ben khuh-**bay**tuh dor 'n (hont/adduh).*
   I've been stung. I've been bitten by a (dog/adder).

7. *Bentoo khuh-vaksin**ayr**d taykhen **tay**ta-nuss?*
   Have you been vaccinated against tetanus?

1. *Ik **naym** dit khen-**ayss**middel rayghel-**maa**tukh.*
   I take this medicine regularly.

2. ***Kun**too-muh 'n **vors**-khrift khayvuh, ashoo-**bleeft**?*
   Can you give me a prescription, please?

3. *Oo moot **nukht**er blayvuh./ Oo makh neets **ay**tuh/**drink**uh.*
   You must fast./ You must not eat/drink anything.

4. *Hoo **owt** – bent oo (iss hay/zay)?*
   How old . . . are you (is he/she)?

5. *Ik ben (hay/zay iss) ... yaar.*
   I am (he/she is) ... years old.

6. ***Hoo**-vayl bennik vers-**khul**dukh?*
   How much do I owe you?

een bloed/urine staal
*'n bloot/uw**reen**uh staal*
a blood/urine sample

Dringende gevallen en naar afspraak
Emergencies and by appointment

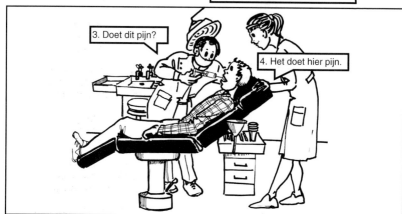

1. Ik heb kiespijn.
2. Kan ik een afspraak maken (so spoedig mogelijk)?
3. Doet dit pijn?
4. Het doet hier pijn.

1. *Ik hep **keess**-payn.*
   I've got toothache.
2. *Kannik 'n **af**-spraak **maak**uh (zo **spoo**dukh **moa**khuh-lukk)?*
   Can I make an appointment (as soon as possible)?

3. *Doot-dit **payn**?*
   Does that hurt?
4. *Hut-doot **heer** payn.*
   It hurts here.

Taking medicine	**Essential information**	I'm ...	*ik ben ...*

... maal per dag
... times a day

allergisch voor (peniciline)
*al-**airk**hiss vor (paynissi-**lee**nuh)*
allergic to (penicillin)

elke ... uur
every ... hours

ik ben zwanger
*ik ben **zvang**-er*
ik ben pregnant

ik heb astma
ik hep assma
I have asthma

voor/na maaltijd
before/after meals

ik lijd aan ...
ik layt aan ...
I'm ...

epilepsie/ suikerziekte
*epi-**lep**see/ **suh**(oo)ker-zeektuh*
epileptic/ diabetic

's morgens/'s avonds
in the morning/evening

gedurende ... dagen
for ... days

ik heb een hoge bloeddruk
*ik hep 'n hoakhuh **bloot**-druk*
I have high blood pressure

indien u pijn heeft
in case of pain

ik heb problemen met m'n hart
*ik hep prob-**lay**muh met-mun **haart***
I have heart trouble

98.6°F = 37°C

de **enkel**
*duh **enk**ul*
the Ankle

de **blindedarm**
*duh **blind**uh-darm*
the Appendix

het **bot**
hut bott
the Bone

de **arm**
duh arrm
the Arm

de **rug**
duh rukh
the Back

de **darmen**
duh darmuh
the Bowels

de **borst**
duh borst
the Chest

het **oor**
hut or
the Ear

de **elleboog**
*duh **ell**uh-bookh*
the Elbow

het **oog**/de **ogen**
hut oakh/duh oakhuh
the Eye/the Eyes

de **vinger**
duh ving-er
the Finger

de **voet**
duh voot
the Foot

de **klier**
duh kleer
the Gland

Mijn ... doet pijn.
*mayn ... doot **payn***
My ... hurts.

de **hand**
duh hant
the Hand

het **hoofd**
hut hoaft
the Head

het **hart**
hut haart
the Heart

de **heup**
duh hurp
the Hip

de **knie**
duh k(uh)nee
the Knee

het **been**
hut bayn
the Leg

de **spierband**
*duh **speer**bant*
the Ligament

de **long**
duh long
the Lung

de **mond**
duh mont
the Mouth

de **spier**
duh speer
the Muscle

de **hals**
duh halss
the Neck

de **zenuw**
*duh **zay**nuw*
the Nerve

de **neus**
duh nurss
the Nose

de **rib**
duh rip
the Rib

de **schouder**
*duh **skhow**-der*
the Shoulder

de **maag**
duh maakh
the Stomach

de **keel**
duh kayl
the Throat

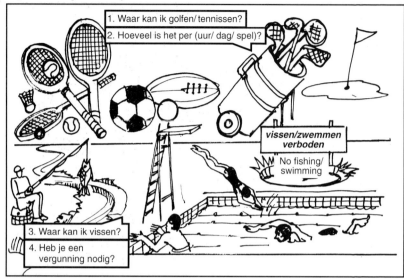

1. **Vaar** *kannik golfuh/ ten-**iss**uh?*
   Where can I play golf/ tennis?

2. **Hoo**-*vayl iss-hut per (uwr/ dakh/ spell)?*
   How much is it per (hour/ day/ game)?

3. **Vaar** *kannik vissuh?*
   Where can I go fishing?

4. *Hep-yuh 'n ver-**khunn**ing **noad**ukh?*
   Do you need a permit?

Mag ik een ... huren?	**Wat is uw schoenmaat?**
Makh-ik 'n ... huwruh?	*Vat-iss oo s'**khoon** maat?*
Can I hire ...?	What's your shoe size?

golfclubs	**een paar schaatsen**	**een surfplank**
golf kluwbs	*'n paar s'khaatsuh*	*'n **surf**-plank*
some Golf Clubs	a pair of Skates	a Surfboard

Waar kan ik ...?	**paardrijden**
Vaar kannik ...?	*paart-rayduh*
Where can I go ...?	Riding

schaatsen	**zwemmen**	**waterskiën**	**(wind)surfen**
s'haatsuh	*zvemmuh*	*vaater skee-uh*	*(vint)-surfuh*
Skating	Swimming	Water Skiing	(Wind)Surfing

1. Wat speelt vanavond in (de bioscoop/het theater)?
2. Graag twee kaartjes voor (zaterdag avond).
3. Wanneer begint de voorstelling?
4. Welke prijs?
5. Zo'n ... .

1. *Vat **spaylt** van-**aav**ont in (duh bee-o **skoap**/hut tay-**ar**ter)?*
   What's on at (the cinema/the theatre) this evening?

2. *Hraakh **tvay kaart**-yuss vor **zaat**erdakh **aav**ont.*
   Two tickets for (Saturday* evening), please.

3. *Van-**ayr** buh-**khint** duh **vor**stelling?*
   When does the performance start?

4. *Velkuh **prayss**?*
   What price

5. *Zoan ...*
   That's ...

1. Is er hier een disco?
2. Ik wil graag naar ...

1. Iss-er heer ('n disco)?
   Is there (a disco) here?

2. *Ik vil **hraakh** naar ...*
   I'd like to go to ...

een concert	**een popconcert**	**een voetbalmatch**
*'n kon-**sairt***	*'n pop kon-**sairt***	*'n **voot** b-al match*
a Concert	a Pop Concert	a Football Match
vanavond	**morgen**	**vrijdag**
*van-**aav**ont*	*mor**khuh***	*vray**dakh***
Tonight	Tomorrow	on Friday*

*days p.94

1. Heeft u informatie over …?

2. Wat zijn de bezienswaardigheden heer?

4. Wanneer is het museum geopend?

3. Er is het kasteel, het museum, de oude stad …

5. Het museum is elke dag open, van … tot …

Waar is … de V.V.V. *duh vayvayvay* [NL]
Vaar iss … het Bureau voor Toerisme [B]
hut buwro vor too-rismuh
Where is … the Tourist Office?

Museums may be closed on Mondays.

1. *Hayft-oo infor-**maat**see over…?*
   Have you any information about …?

2. ***Vat** zayn duh buh-**zeenss-vaar**dukh-hayduh heer?*
   What is there to see here?.

3. *Er iss hut ka-**stayl**, hut muw-**zayum**, duh ow-duh **stat**…*
   There's the castle, the museum, the old town …

4. *Van-**ayr** iss hut muw-**zay**um khuh-**oap**ent?*
   When is the museum open?

5. *Hut muw-**zay**um iss **elk**uh dakh **oap**uh, van … tot …*
   It's open every day, from … to …

Tentoonstelling
Exhibition

(vrije) Toegang
Entrance (free)

Uitgang
Exit/Way out

1. Is er een Engelstalige gids?

2. Is er korting voor (kinderen/ studenten/ a.o.w.)?

3. Het is gratis.

4. Kunt u me enkele wandelingen aanraden

1. *Iss-er 'n **eng**-els-**taa**likhuh **khits**?*
   Is there an English-speaking guide?

2. *Iss-er **kor**ting vor (kinderuh/ stuw**dent**uh/ aa-oh-**vay**)?*
   Is there any reduction for (children/ students/ pensioners)?

3. *Hut-iss **khraa**tiss.*
   It's free.

4. ***Kun**too-muh **enkel**uh **vand**erlinguh **aan**raaduh?*
   Can you recommend any walks round here?

1. **Dakh**, hoo **khaat**-hut?
   Hello. How are you?

2. **Khoot**, dankoo. En **oo**?
   Fine, thanks - and you?

3. Mayn **naam** iss ... Hoo hayt **oo**?
   My name is ... What's yours?

4. Dit-iss mayn ... man/vrow, zoan/dokhter,
   vreent/vreen**din**.
   This is my ... husband/wife, son/daughter,
   friend [m/f].

5. **Prett**ikh mettoo **kenn**istuh maakuh.
   Pleased to meet you.

6. **Da**-akh.
   Goodbye.

1. Hallo! Mayn **naam** iss ...
   Hi! My name's ...

2. Dit-iss mun (**broo**-er/zuss).
   This is my (brother/sister).

3. Hep **yay broo**-erss en **zush**uh?
   Have you any brothers and sisters?

4. Hoo **owt** ben **yay**?
   How old are you?

5. Ik ben der-**teen**.
   I'm 13.*

*Numbers p.131

1. **Iss**-dit oo **air**stuh buz**zook** aan
   (Nayderlant/**Bel**khee-yuh)?
   Is this your first visit to
   (Holland/Belgium)?

2. Ya (nay). Ik **sprayk** 'n klayn bayt-yuh
   nayderlanss.
   Yes (no). I only speak a little Dutch.

3. **Hoo** vint-oo hut **heer**?
   How do you like it here?

4. Ik vint-hut **airkh** lurk.
   I think it's very nice.

5. **Vaar** komt-oo van-**daan**?
   Where are you from?**

6. Ik **voan** in Lonnduh.
   I live in London.

7. **Vat**vor **vairk** dootoo?
   What do you do?

8. Ik ben (stuw-**dent**/ op ruwst).
   I'm (a student/ retired).

9. **Hoo**-lang **blayft**-oo heer?
   How long are you staying here?

10. Ik ver-**trek** (**zaat**erdakh).
    I'm leaving on (Saturday).

*stuw-**dent**uh - fem.
**countries p.92

Accepting an invitation

* informal:
  ben je *ben-yuh*
  wil je *vil-yuh*

1. Bent-oo van-**aav**ont **vray**?
   Are you free this evening?

2. Vilt-oo ayvuh langss-**koam**uh vor 'n
   borrel?
   Would you like to come for a drink?

3. Dat-iss **lurk**. Ya, hraakh.
   That would be nice. Yes, please.

4. Van-**ayr zull**uh-vuh el-**kaar** ont-
   mootuh? Vaar?
   When shall we meet? Where?

Visiting

1. Dag! (Goede avond.) Prettig met u* kennis te maken.
2. Gaat u zitten*.
3. Wat wilt u* drinken? - koffie, een glas wijn, een glasje fris?
4. Neemt u maar. Nog wat?
5. Ja, graag. (Nee, dank u.)
6. Vindt u het lekker?
7. Het is heerlijk!
8. Houdt u* van sport, lezen, dansen, muziek?
9. Ik hou van ...

1. **Dakh**! (Hooyuh **aav**ont!) **Prett**ikh mettoo **kenn**istuh maakuh.
   Hello. Welcome! Pleased to meet you!

2. **Khaat**-oo zittuh.
   Please sit down.

3. Vat **vilt**-oo drinkuh? - koffee, 'n glass **vayn**, 'n glass-yuh **friss**?
   What would you like to drink? - coffee, a glass of wine, a soft drink?

4. **Naymt**-oo maar. Nokh **vat**?
   Please help yourself. A little more?

5. **Ya**, hraakh. (**Nay**, dankoo.)
   Yes, please. (No, thanks.)

6. **Vint**-oo hut **lekk**er?
   Do you like it?

7. Hut-iss **hayr**-lukk!
   It's delicious!

8. **Howt**-oo van dansuh, layzuh, muw-**zeek**, sporrt?
   Do you like dancing, reading, music, sport?

9. Ik **how** van ...
   I like ...

*informal: 1.met je, 2.ga zitten, 3.wil je, 8.hou je

Saying goodbye

2. Kom vlug terug.
1. Dank u wel voor alles. (Ik had) een erg leuke tijd. (We hadden...)
3. Da ... ag. Tot ziens!

1. Dankoo **vel** vor al-uss. (Ik hat) 'n **airkh** lurkuh **tayt**. (Vuh hadduh...)
   Thanks for everything. (I had) a lovely time. (We had ...)

2. Kom **vlukh** ter-**ukh**.
   Come again soon.

3. Da-akh. **Tot** seenss!
   Goodbye!

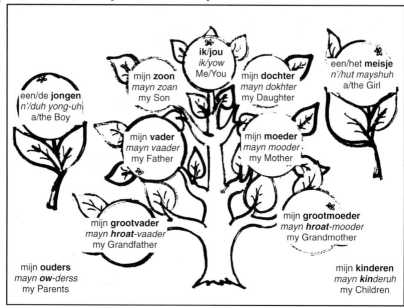

mijn **ouders**
mayn ow-derss
my Parents

mijn **kinderen**
mayn kinderuh
my Children

Countries and nationalities

ik kom uit ...	Nederland	België	Waar komt u vandaan?
ik kom uh(oo)t ...	*nayderlant*	*belkhee-yuh*	*Vaar komt-oo van-daan?*
I come from ...	Netherlands	Belgium	Where are you from?

ik ben (Nederlander / Nederlandse)
ik ben (nayderlanter / nayderlansuh)
I'm Dutch [m/f]

ik ben (Belg/ Belgische)
ik ben (belkh/ bel-khissuh)
I'm Belgian [m/f]

Engeland	**Engels/Engelse**	**Ierland**	**Iers/Ierse**
eng-uh-lant	*eng-elss/eng-elsuh*	*eerlant*	*eerss/eersuh*
England	English	Ireland	Irish

Wales	**Welsh/Welshe**	**Schotland**	**Schots/Schotse**
wales	*welsh/welshuh*	*s'khotlant*	*s'khots/s'khotsuh*
Wales	Welsh	Scotland	Scottish

Canada	**de Verenigde Staten**	**Australië**	**Nieuw-Zeeland**
kana-da	*ver-aynikhduh staatuh*	*ow-straal-yuh*	*new zaylant*
Canada	the USA	Australia	New Zealand

Frankrijk	**Duitsland**	**Luxemburg**	
frank-rayk	*duh(oo)ts-lant*	*luxemburkh*	
France	Germany	Luxembourg	

Pests, theft...

1. Hou op!
2. Ga weg!
3. Laat me gerust!

1. *How op!*
   Stop!
2. *Khaa **vekh**!*
   Go away!
3. ***Laat**muh khuh-**ruwst**!*
   Leave me alone!

... and problems

1. Ik ben (m'n paspoort/ mijn reischeques) kwijt.
2. (Mijn tas) is gestolen.
3. Hoe ziet het er uit? Wat was de inhoud?
4. Waar verblijft u?
5. Kunt u dit formulier invullen.

1. *Ik ben (mun **pass**port/ mun **rayss**-shecks) **kvayt**.*
   I've lost (my passport/ my traveller's cheques).
2. *(Mayn tass) iss khu**stoa**luh.*
   (My bag) has been stolen.
3. ***Hoo** zeet-hut er-**uh**(oo)t?*
   ***Vat**-vass duh **in**howt?*
   What does it look like? What was in it?
4. ***Vaar** ver-**blayft**-oo?*
   Where are you staying?
5. *Kuntoo dit formoo-**leer in**-vulluh.*
   Could you fill in this form.

1. ***Vaar** iss hut po**lit**see buw-**ro**?*
   Where is the police station?
2. ***Kun**too-muh **help**uh?*
   Can you help me?
3. *Ik ben **aan**khuh-**val**luh.*
   I've been attacked.
4. *Ik **hep** khayn **khelt**.*
   I have no money.
5. ***Vat** mootik **doon**?*
   What shall I do?

1. Waar is het politiebureau?
2. Kunt u me helpen?
3. Ik ben aangevallen.
4. Ik heb geen geld.
5. Wat moet ik doen?

naam	**voornaam**	**adres**	**wanneer**	**waar**
naam	***vor**naam*	*add**ress***	*van-**ayr***	*vaar*
Surname	First name	Address	When	Where

}?

gisteren	vandaag	morgen
khisteruh	*van-daakh*	*morkhuh*
Yesterday	Today	Tomorrow

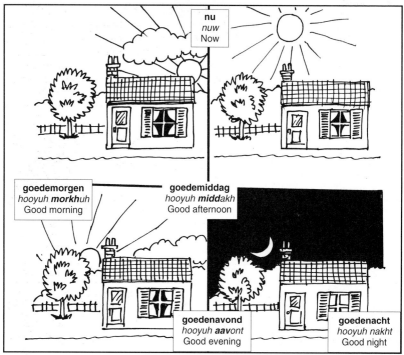

nu
nuw
Now

goedemorgen
hooyuh morkhuh
Good morning

goedemiddag
hooyuh middakh
Good afternoon

goedenavond
hooyuh aavont
Good evening

goedenacht
hooyuh nakht
Good night

's morgens	's middags	's avonds	's nachts
smorkhunss	*smiddakhs*	*saavonts*	*snakhs*
in the Morning	in the Afternoon	in the Evening	at Night

Days of the week – *de week* – *vayk*

maandag
maandakh
Monday

vrijdag
vraydakh
Friday

dinsdag
dinsdakh
Tuesday

zaterdag
zaaterdakh
Saturday

woensdag
vunsdakh
Wednesday

donderdag
donderdakh
Thursday

sondag
zondakh
Sunday

Seasons, months, weather

in de winter	induh vinter	in Winter

Vrolijk Kerstfeest!
*vro-lukk **kairst**-fayst*
Merry Christmas!

het sneeuwt
*hut **snay**-(uw)t*
it's Snowing

Gelukkig Nieuwjaar!
*khuh-**lukk**ukh new **yaar***
Happy New Year

december	**januari**	**februari**
*day-**sem**ber*	*yannoo-**aar**ee*	*faybroo-**aar**ee*
December	January	February

in de lente	induh lentuh	in Spring

Pasen
paassuh
Easter

het regent
*hut **ray**-khent*
it's Raining

het waait
hut v-eye-t
it's Windy

maart	**april**	**mei**
marrt	*app-**ril***	*may*
March	April	May

in de zomer	induh zoamer	in Summer

het is zonnig
hut-iss zonnukh
it's Sunny

ik heb het warm
*ik hep-hut **varm***
I'm Hot

juni	**juli**	**het is erg warm**	**augustus**
yuwnee	*yuwlee*	*hut-iss **airkh** varm*	*ow-**gust**us*
June	July	it's Hot	August

in de herfst	induh hairfst	in Autumn/Fall

het mist
hut mist
it's Foggy

het is koud
hut-iss kowt
it's Cold

ik heb het koud
*ik hep-hut **kowt***
I'm Cold

september	**oktober**	**november**
*sep-**tem**ber*	*ok-**tob**er*	*no-**vem**ber*
September	October	November

Things: nouns Most nouns are common gender but some are neuter.

A For one item - **singular** (s.), use *een: een dag* a day *een boek* a book

The For common nouns use *de*, neuter *het*. All ending in *-je* are neuter.
de dag the day   *het boek* the book   *het kaartje* the ticket

Plural (pl.) For more than one item, both genders use *de*.
de dagen the days   *de boeken* the books   *de kaartjes* the tickets

Long/short vowels To preserve their meaning, nouns must keep the same sound in the plural as they had in the singular.

In a monosyllabic word with one vowel and ending in one consonant, the vowel is short, eg *man* (man). Following it by *-en* (to make it plural), would make the vowel long. To keep it short, the middle consonant is doubled: *mannen*.

Double vowels are long, eg *maan* (moon). Adding *-en* (the plural) would make this *maanen*, but since the *a* is already long (being followed by a single consonant), the second *a* is unnecessary and it becomes *manen*.

Other examples: kat/katten   bed/bedden   laan/lanen   boom/bomen

Most nouns ending in *-s* or *-f* change this to *-z* or *-v* respectively:
          huis   huizen house/s   *brief   brieven* letter/s

Some change the vowel: *stad steden* town/s   *schip schepen* ship/s

Most ending in unstressed *-aar, -el, -em, -en, -er* and all ending in *-je* add *-s:*
          tafel   tafels table/s   *kaartje   kaartjes* ticket/s

Many nouns of foreign origin end in a vowel. If this is *a, o, u* or *y,* add an apostrophe:
          taxi   taxi's taxi/s   *baby   baby's* baby/babies

Describing words: adjectives As in English, the adjective usually precedes the noun it describes, adding -e in both singular and plural:
goed (good): *een goede man* a good man   *goede mannen* good men

The adjective does <u>not</u> add *-e* if:

a) it follows the noun: *de man is goed*
b) the noun is neuter s. and no article (a/the) is used: *koud water   geen geld*
c) the noun is neuter s. and is preceded by *een* (a), *elk/ieder* (each),
   veel (much), *welk* (which) or *zulk* (such):
   welk spoor (het spoor) but *welke maat (de maat)*
   geen (no) never changes

Mine, yours: possessives

		Except for *ons* , these do not change:	
my *mijn*	his, its *zijn*	our *ons/onze*	their *hun*
your *jouw/*uw*	her *haar*	your *jullie*	

ons: neuter sing.; *onze:* common sing., all plurals

You, your: it is best to use *u* and *uw* whether talking to one person or several, since *jij/je*, *jouw* and *jullie* are for children and people you know well.

Action: Verbs (shown in dictionaries in the 'to' form). 'Regular' verbs: remove *-en*, leaving the stem to which endings are then added, eg *werken* to work:

ik werk	*hij/zij/het werkt*	*ik werkte* (I worked)
*jij/*u werkt*	*wij/jullie/zij werken*	*ik heb gewerkt* (I have worked)

to be	*zijn*	**to have**	*hebben*
I am	*ik ben*	I have	*ik heb*
you are	*jij/*u bent*	you have	*jij/*u hebt*
he/she/it is	*hij/zij/het is*	he/she/it has	*hij/zij/het heeft*
we/you/they are	*wij/jullie/zij zijn*	we/you/they have	*wij/jullie/zij hebben*
I have been...	*ik ben... geweest*	I have had...	*ik heb... gehad*
we have been	*wij zijn... geweest*	we have had	*wij hebben... gehad*

to go	*gaan*	**to want**	*willen*
I go	*ik ga*	I want	*ik wil*
you go	*jij/*u gaat*	you want	*jij/*u wilt*
he/she/it goes	*hij/zij/het gaat*	he/she/it wants	*hij/zij/het wil*
we/you/they go	*wij/jullie/zij gaan*	we/you/they want	*wij/jullie/zij willen*
I went/have been...	*ik ging/ben... gegaan*	I wanted	*ik wilde*
we " " "	*wij gingen/zijn... gegaan*	we wanted	*wij wilden*

to be able	*kunnen*	**to have to**	*moeten*
I can	*ik kan*	I must	*ik moet*
you can	*jij/*u kunt*	you must	*jij/*u moet*
he/she/it can	*hij/zij/het kan*	he/she/it must	*hij/zij/het moet*
we/you/they can	*wij/jullie/zij kunnen*	we/you/they must	*wij/jullie/zij moeten*
I was able to	*ik kon*	I had to	*ik moest*
we were able to	*wij konden*	we had to	*wij moesten*

Saying no   Put *niet* after the verb: *het werkt niet* - it's not working.

Questions   Take a statement: *u spreekt Engels* - you speak English.
Reverse it: *spreekt u Engels?* - do you speak English?

A - *een* for all nouns. **The** singular - *de* or *het*; in the plural all use de.
Compound nouns take the gender of the second word.
m - masculine version, *f* - feminine, *s.o.* - someone, *s.t.* - something
oud/e, wit/witte alternative forms, mostly adjectives.

Stress: first syllable unless indicated by underlining (second syllable after the prefixes *be-, er-, ge-, her-, ont-, ver-*).
Food: Dutch names are given in the Menu Guide only.
Words identical to both languages are shown only in the English section.

Dutch-English

A

aan to, on, at, of
aanbevelen to recommend
de **aanbieding** special offer
aangevallen attacked (**aanvallen** attack)
aangeven to declare; **iets aan te geven** anything to declare
de **aankomst** arrival; **aangekomen** arrived (**aankomen** arrive)
de **aankoopsom** purchase price
de **aannemer** builder
aanpassen to try on
aanraden to recommend
de **aansluiting** connection
de **aansteker** *-s* lighter/s
het **aantal** number of
acht eight
achter behind; **~laten** to leave *(s.t.)*
de **adder** *-s* adder/s
het **adres** *adressen* address/es
afhalen to collect
afgesloten rijweg road closed
afnemend/e decreasing
de **afrit** motorway exit
de **afsluiting** *-en* fence/s
de **afspraak** *-spraken* appointment/s; **~maken** make an a-; **na ~** by a-
afstappen to get off
de **afval** rubbish, trash
het **afwasproduct** washing-up liquid
al all; already
alcoholvrij non-alcoholic
alleen only; **~ op** only on; **~ voor voetgangers** pedestrians only
allergisch allergic, *voor* to
alles everything, all
als as, if, when; **~ op** as on
alsjeblieft, alstublieft here you are
altijd always
Amerika America; **Amerikaans**/e American *m/f*
ander/e other; **~e richtingen** o-directions; **~half** one and a half

anders: niets ~ nothing else; different; **~validen** disabled
de **anti-vries** antifreeze
annuleren to cancel
het **antwoord** *-en* reply -lies (**antwoorden** reply)
a.o.w.: aan de ~ on a pension
het **appartement** *-en* apartment/s, flat/s
de **apotheek** *-theken* chemist/s
de **arts** *-en* doctor/s
de **asperges** asparagus
de **aspirine** aspirin
de **assemblage** assembly *machine*
het **astma** asthma
a.u.b. - *alsjeblieft, alstublieft* please
aubergines aubergines, eggplants
augustus August
de **auto** *auto's* car/s; **met de ~** by car; **verhuur** car hire; **~lweg/snelweg** motor/freelway
het **autogas** LPG
de **automaat** ticket machine, automat
de **avond** *-en* evening/s; het **~maal** e-meal; **'s avonds** in the e-
de **azijn** vinegar

B

het **baantje**, de **baan** job
de **babyvoeding** baby food
het **bad** *-en* bath/s; de **~kamer** bathroom
de **bagage** luggage; **~kluizen** l- lockers; het **~rek** l- carrier; de **~riem** l- strap
bakboord port *(side)*
bakken to cook, bake
de **bakker** *-s* baker/s; de **banket~** cake shop
de **bal** *ballen* ball/s
de **band** *-en* tyre/s, de **~druk** tyre pressure
de **bank** *-en* bank/s; de **~kaart** b- card
de **batterij** *-en* battery -ries
het **bed** *bedden* bed/s; **kinder~** child's b-
de **bediening** service; **inclusief ~** s-included
bedraagt amounts to; het **bedrag** amount (**bedragen** amount to)

het	**bedrijf** industry; company; **dochter~** subsidiary c-
het	**been** *benen* leg/s
een	**beetje** a little
	begint begins; het **begin** beginning (**beginnen** begin)
	begrijpen to understand
	behalve except
de	**behanger** decorator
	behoren to belong; **aan wie behoort...** who does... belong to
de	**beker** *-s* mug/s
	belangrijk/e important
de	**belasting** *-en* tax/es
	Belg/Belgische Belgian *m/f;* **België** Belgium
	bellen to phone *(ik bel)*
ik	**ben** I am; **bent** is/are *(zijn* - be)
	beneden below; down, downstairs; de **~verdieping** ground floor
de	**benzine** gas, petrol; het **~station** filling station
de	**berg** *-en* hill/s
	beroemd famous
	beschikken over to have, be equipped with
	besluiten to decide (**besloten** - decided)
de	**bestelling** *-en* order/s; **op ~** made to order; **~ plaatsen** place an o-; de **~snota** o- form (**bestellen** - order; ik **bestelde** - I ordered)
	betaal, hier betalen pay! (**betalen** - pay)
	betekenen to mean
	beu: ik ben het ~ I'm fed up
	bezet occupied; engaged
de	**bezienswaardigheden** the sights
het	**bezoek** *-en* visit/s; het **~adres** address for visitors; **~ers** visitors (**bezoeken** - visit)
	BG - *Begane Grond* ground floor
het	**bier** *-en* beer/s; **~ van het vat** draught beer
	bij by, at; **~ u** at your house/place; **~ vergissing** if you make a mistake
de	**bij** *-en* bee/s
	bijna almost
	binnen inside, within; de **~band** inner tube; **~lands/e** inland, internal
de	**bioscoop** cinema, movie theater
	blauw/e blue
	blijven to stay; **blijf aan de lijn** please hold
het	**blik** *blikken* can/s, tin/s; de **~opener** c- opener
de	**blindedarm** appendix
het	**bloed** blood; **hoge ~druk** high b- pressure; het **~ staal** b- sample

de	**bloem** *-en* flower/s
de	**bocht** *-en* bend/s; **gevaarlijke ~** dangerous b-
de	**boerderij** *-en* farm/s
het	**boek** *-en* book/s; de **~handel** b-shop; de **~ing** b-ing
het	**bolletje** *-s* scoop/s
	bonbons sweets
het	**bonnetje** receipt
de	**boodschap** message
de	**boom** *bomen* tree/s
de	**boot** *boten* boat/s
het	**bord** *-en* plate/s; board; sign
de	**borrel** *(alcoholic)* drink
de	**borst** chest
de	**borstel** *-s* brush/es
het	**bos** wood, forest; **~bessen** bil/blueberries
het	**bot** *botten* bone/s
de	**boter** butter; de **~ham** open sandwich
de	**bougie** *-s* spark/glow plug/s
	bouwen to build
	boven above, upstairs
de	**braadpan** *-pannen* frying pan/s
de	**brandweer** fire brigade
	breed wide
	breken to break
	brengen to bring
de	**brief** *brieven* letter/s; de **brievenbus** postbox
de	**bril** glasses (spectacles)
de	**broek** pair of trousers; de **~sriem** *-en* belt/s
de	**broer** *-s* brother/s
de	**bromfiets** moped
het	**brood** bread; het **broodje** *-s* roll/s
de	**brug** *bruggen* bridge/s; de **~ over** over the b-
	bruin/e brown; het **bruin café** student-type pub
	BTW - *Belasting Toegevoegde Waarde* VAT
	buiten outside; **~ gebruik** out of order; de **~boordmotor** outboard motor
het	**buitenland** abroad; **~er** *-s* foreigner/s; **~s/e** foreign
de	**bukking** kipper
het	**bureau** office; **~ voor toerisme** tourist o-
	buurt: in de ~ nearby
de	**bus** *bussen* bus/es, de **~halte** bus stop; het **~station** bus station
	b.v. - *bij voorbeeld* for example

C

de	**cabine** *-s* cabin/s
het	**cadeau** *-s* present/s

de **camping** *-s* campsite/s
de **centrale verwarming** central heating
het **centrum** centre; **stads~** town centre
de **chips** crisps *Br*, chips *Am*
de **chocolade** chocolate; het **~ijsje** c-
  ice cream; de **warme ~melk** hot c-
de **collega** *collega's* colleague/s
de **commissie** commission
het **condoom** *-domen* condom/s
  constipatie constipation
de **contactsleutel** ignition key
de **crème voor de billetjes** nappy cream

D

  daar there
  dag hello, good day; goodbye
de **dag** *-en* day/s; **per ~** per day
  dagelijks daily
de **dagkaart** *-en* all-day ticket/s
de **dagschotel** *-s* today's special/s
het **dak** *-en* roof/s
  dames ladies'; de **~slip** briefs
  dan then; than
  dank u thank you; **dankbaar** grateful
  (**danken** thank)
  dansen to dance, dancing
de **darmen** bowels
  dat that; **~ daar** that one
de **datum** *-s* date/s
de **decafé** decaffeinated coffee
het **deel** *delen* part/s
  defect broken down, faulty
het **dek** deck
het **dekbed** eiderdown
de **deken** *-s* blanket/s
  denken to think; **dat denk ik** I think
  so; **dat denk ik niet** I don't...
de **deur** *-en* door/s
  deze this, this one, these
voor **dia's** for slides *film*
de **diaree** diarrhoea
  dicht turned off, closed
  dichtbij near; **dichtstbijzijnde**
  nearest
  die that, those; who, which
de **dienstregeling** *-en* timetable/s
het **dier** *-en* animal/s; de **~entuin** zoo
  dik/dikke fat, thick
de **dijk** *-en* dike/s
het **diner** dinner *evening*
het **ding** *-en* thing/s
  dinsdag Tuesday; **di.** Tues.
de **directeur** *-en* manager/s
de **diskette** *-n* computer disk/s
  dit this/these
  diverse (**soorten**) different (kinds of)
de **dochter** *-s* daughter/s; het **~bedrijf**
  subsidiary company
ik **doe** I do; **u doet** you do;

het **doet pijn** it hurts (**doen** - do)
de **dokter** *-s* doctor/s
  donderdag Thursday; **do.** Thurs.
  donker dark; **~blauw** dark blue
  doodlopende weg no through road
  door through, because of; **~gaand**
  verkeer through traffic
  doorgebakken well-done *food*
  doorgeven to pass on
het **dorp** *-en* village/s
  dorst: **ik heb ~** I'm thirsty *(dorst*
  hebben)
de **douane** customs; de **~beambte**
  c- officer
de **douche** *-s* shower/s
  draai turn! **~ dicht/open** off/on
  (**draaien** turn)
het **drankje** *-s* drink/s
  drie three; **~ kleuren** three colours
  dringend urgent
  drinken to drink
de **drogist** drugstore
  droog/droge dry
de **druk** pressure; **hoge/lage ~** high/low p-
het **druk hebben** to be busy
  drukken press, to press
  Duits/e German *m/f;* **Duitsland**
  Germany
  duur expensive; **te ~** too e-
  duren to take time, to last; **het duurt**
  it takes/lasts
  duwen push, to push
de **dweil** floorcloth
de **-dwarsstraat** cross-, side-street

E

  ebbe en vloed low and high tide
  echt/e real, genuine
  een a, one; **~maal** once;
  ~persoonkamer single room;
  ~richtingsverkeer one-way
  traffic; **één** one
de **eenheid** *-heden* unit/s
  eerst/e first; **~volgend** next; **eerste**
  Kerstdag Christmas Day
het **eet|café** café; de **~kamer, ~zaal**
  dining room
  eigen own; **~gemaakt** home made;
  ~lijk actual/ly; **~ weg** private road
het **eiland** *-en* island/s
het **einde** end; **~lijk** finally; de
  eindproducten finished products
  eindigen to finish; het **eindigt** it
  finishes
de **elektricien** electrician
de **elektriciteit** electricity; de **~skast** fuse
  box
  elektrisch electric; het **~e systeem**
  the electrics *car*

elk/e each, every; **elke... uur** every... hours; **elkaar** each other
de **elleboog** -*bogen* elbow/s
en and
Engels/e English; ~**man**/**Engelse** E. man/woman; ~**talig**/e E-speaking; **Engeland** England
de **enkel** -*s* ankle/s
enkel/e single, a few; **enkele reis** single journey
de **enveloppe** -*n* envelope/s
enz. - *enzovoort* etc
de **epilepsie** epilepsy
er is/**zijn** there is/are *(zijn* be)
erg very; **hoe ~** how dreadful
eten to eat, eating; het ~ food
even just, just as, equally
eventueel possible
exclusief exclusive, not included
het **exemplaar** -*plaren* copy/copies

F
de **fabriek** -*en* factory -ries
faciliteiten facilities
de **factuur** *facturen* invoice/s (**factureren** invoice)
de **familie** -*s* family -lies; de ~**kamer** f-room
favoriet favourite
februari February
het **feest** -*en* party -ties; (**publieke**) ~**dagen** (public) holidays
de **fiets** -*en* bicycle/s, ~**ers** cyclists; het ~**pad** cycle path (**fietsen** cycle)
fijne en bereide vleeswaren delicatessen
de **file** traffic jam; ~**vrij** road clear
de **film** -*s* film/s, movie/s; het ~**rolletje** *camera* film
de **firma** *firma's* company -nies
de **flat** -*s* apartment/s, flat/s
de **fles** *flessen*, het **flesje** bottle/s; de ~**senopener** b- opener
het **formulier** -*en* form/s
het **fornuis** stove, cooker
de **foto** *foto's* photo/s; het ~**toestel** camera
Frankrijk France; **Frans**/e French *m/f*
de **fris** -*dranken* soft drink/s
frites chips/fries
het **fruit** fruit; het ~**sap** fruit juice

G
gaat goes; **hoe ~ het** how are you; **ga weg!** go away! (**gaan** - go; *ik ga)*
de **garage** -*s* garage/s
het **garen** thread

het **gas** gas; de ~**fles** gas bottle; het ~**lichtje** pilot light
Geachte Heer, Mevrouw Dear Sir or Madam
ge- *see also under next letter* (verb past tense, p.97)
gebakken baked, fried *(bakken* bake, fry)
gebarsten cracked *(barsten* crack)
gebeten bitten; *door* by *(bijten* bite)
gebeurd: wat is ~ what's happened
het **gebied** -*en* area/s
geblokkeerd blocked *(blokkeren* block)
gebogen bent *(buigen* bend)
het **gebouw** -*en* building/s
gebroken broken *(breken* break)
gebruik: buiten ~ out of order; **voor uitwendig ~** for external use; ~**saanwijzing** instructions
gebruiken to use, take *eg sugar*
gedurende for, during
geef/geeft give/s; **het geeft niet** it doesn't matter *(geven* give)
geel/gele yellow
geen no, not a/any; ~ **toegang** no entry
gegrild grilled *(grillen* grill)
geïnfecteerd infected *(infecteren* infect)
het **geld** money; de ~**automaat** cash dispenser
geldt niet voor doesn't apply to; **geldig** valid; (**gelden** apply to, be valid)
geleden ago
gelijk hebben to be right; **ik heb**/**u hebt gelijk** I'm/you're right
de **geluidsdemper** silencer
gelukkig happy; **G- Nieuwjaar** Happy New Year
gemakkelijk easy
het **gemeentehuis** town hall
gemist missed *(missen* miss)
het **geneesmiddel** -*en* medicine/s
genoeg enough
geopend open *(openen* open)
de **gepensioneerde** -*n* pensioner/s
het **gerecht** -*en* dish/es *menu*
gerepareerd repaired *(repareren* repair)
gereserveerd reserved *(reserveren* reserve)
gescheiden divorced
gesloten closed; **voor auto's ~** c- to motor vehicles *(sluiten* close)
gesmaakt: heeft het u ~ did you enjoy it *(smaken* taste)
gestoken stung *(steken* sting)

gestolen stolen *(stelen* steal)
getrouwd married
het **gevaar** danger
gevaarlijk dangerous; ~**e afdaling/bocht** d- hill/bend
gevaccineerd tegen vaccinated against
het **geval** -*vallen* case/s, event/s
geven to give *(ik geef)*
gevraagd/e requested *(vragen* ask, request)
het **gewicht** weight
gewoon ordinary; ~**lijk** usual
gezellig pleasant, friendly
het **gezicht** -*en* face/s
de **gids** -*en* guide/s
ginds over there
gisteren yesterday
glad slippery; ~**de weg** s- road
het **glas** *glazen* glass/es
de **gloeilamp** -*en* light bulb/s
gluten-vrij gluten-free
goed/e good, OK; **goedendag** hello, good day
goede|middag good afternoon, ~**morgen** g- morning; ~**navond** g- evening, ~**nacht** g- night
goedkoop cheap; **goedkoper** cheaper
golfen to play golf
de **goot** *goten* drain/s
de **gootsteen** sink
het **gordijn** -*en* curtain/s; de ~**stang** c- rail
goudkleurig golden
graag please, with pleasure
de **gracht** -*en* canal/s *narrow, in towns*
gratis free
grijs grey
groen/e green; de **groente** -*n* vegetable/s
de **groep** -*en* group/s; batch (**producten** of production)
de **grond** ground; de ~**stoffen** raw materials
groot/grote big; **Groot-Brittanië** Gt. Britain; de ~**vader/moeder** grandfather/mother; de **grote markt** main square
de **GSM** mobile phone
het **gymnasium** *gymnasia* high school/s

H

h hour *abbr.*
haar/d'r her
het **haar** hair
de **haard** fireplace
de **haardroger** hair dryer
ik **had, we hadden** I/we had *(hebben* have)

half/halve half; half past; ~**volle** semi-skimmed
de **hals** neck
de **halte** -*n* stop/s
de **hamer** hammer
de **hand** -*en* hand/s; de ~**doek** towel; ~**schoenen** gloves; **wat is er aan de ~** what's the matter
hangen to hang; **het hangt af van...** it depends on...
het **hart** heart
hartelijk warm; ~ **dank** many thanks
de **haven** -*s* harbour/s; de ~**meester** h-master
ik **heb** I have; **we hebben** we h-; **ik heb... nodig** I need... (**hebben** have)
de **hectare** -*n* hectare/s *(c. 2.5 acres)*
heeft has/have *(hebben* have)
heel/hele whole, all
heen en terug there and back; return ticket
de **heer** Mr, sir
heerlijk lovely, delicious
heet very hot; is/are called (**heten** be called)
de **helm** -*en* helmet/s
helpen to help
hem/'m him
het **hemd** -*en* shirt/s
Hemelvaartsdag Ascension Day *(40 after Easter)*
hen them
heren men's; m- toilets; de ~**slip** m-briefs
de **herfst** autumn, fall
herhalen to repeat
het/'t it; the *neuter*
de **heup** -*en* hip/s
de **heuvel** -*s* hill/s
hier here
hij/ie he
hoe how; ~ **lang** h- long; ~**veel** h-much/many
de **hoed** -*en* hat/s
de **hoek** -*en* corner/s
het **hoeft niet** it doesn't need (**be-/hoeven** need)
hoesten to cough, coughing
Hollands/e Dutch
de **hond** -*en* dog/s
honger hebben to be hungry
het **hoofd** -*en* head/s; het ~**bureau** h-office; het ~**gerecht** -*en* main course/s; de ~**kraan** stopcock; het ~**kussen** -*s* pillow/s; de ~**pijn** h-ache; het ~**postkantoor** main post office; de ~**stad** capital; de ~**verkeersweg** main road

hoog/hoge high, tall; **hoge druk** high pressure
hoogachtend yours faithfully
de **hooikoorts** hay fever
ik **hoop** I hope; **dat ~ ik** (**niet**) I hope so/not (**hopen** hope)
hou op! stop, stop it! *(ophouden* stop doing)
het **huis** *huizen* house/s; de **~bewaarder** hostel manager
de **hulp** help; **eerste ~post** first aid post
hun/hen them; their
huren to hire, rent; **te huur** for hire

I

het **idee** *ideeën* idea/s
de **identiteitskaart** *-en* identity card/s
iedereen everyone
iemand someone
iets some/anything; **~ aan te geven** anything to declare
ik/'k I
het **ijs** ice; **met ~** with i-; **~blokken** i-blocks; het **ijsje** i- cream; de **~kast** fridge
in in
inbegrepen included; **niet ~** excluded
inchecken to check in
inclusief included
indien in case; **~ u pijn heeft** in case of pain
indienen: een klacht ~ to make a complaint
indrukken to press
de **industrie** *-s* industry -ries; het **~terrein** industrial area
de **informatie** information; *over* about
de **ingang** *-en* entrance/s
ingewikkeld complicated
inhaalverbod no overtaking
de **inhoud** contents
de **inlichtingen** information point
de **insecten|beet** *-beten* insect bite/s; het **~verwerend middel** i- repellant
instappen to board, boarding
interessant/e interesting
ik **interesseer me voor** I'm interested in (**zich interesseren** be interested)
i.p.v. - *in plaats van* instead of
is is *(zijn* be)

J

ja yes; **jawel** yes, indeed
het **jaar** *jaren* year/s, years old; de **jaaromzet** turnover
het **jacht** *-en* yacht/s; de **~haven** marina
jammer genoeg unfortunately
januari January
de **jas** *jassen* coat/s; het **jasje** *-n* jacket/s

jazeker certainly; yes, of course
je you *familiar;* **-je** little –
de **jeans** jeans
jenever gin
de **jeugdherberg** *-en* youth hostel/s
jong/e young; early; de **jongen** *-s* boy/s
jou/je you
jouw/jullie your *fam. s/pl*
juli July
juni June
de **jurk** *-en* dress/es

K

de **kaars** *-en* spark/glow plug/s
de **kaart** *-en* map/s
het **kaartje** *-s* ticket/s; visiting card/s
de **kaas** cheese; **belegen ~** mature c-; **oude ~** old c-
de **kabel** *-s* cable/s
de **kade** quay
het **kado** *-s* present/s
kalm/e calm
de **kam** *kammen* comb/s
de **kamer** *-s* room/s; **~ vrij** rooms available
de **kampeerauto** *-auto's* motor caravan/s
de **kampplaats** pitch *campsite*
ik **kan** I can *(kunnen* be able)
de **kan** *kannen* jug/s
het **kanaal** *kanalen* canal/s *wide;* het **K-** the Channel; de **K-tunnel** C-Tunnel
het **kantoor** *kantoren* office/s
de **kapel** *kapellen* chapel/s
kapot broken
de **kas, kassa** cash desk; de **kassier** cashier
de **kast** *-en* cupboard/s, closet/s
het **kasteel** *kastelen* castle/s
de **kat** *katten* cat/s
de **kathedraal** *-dralen* cathedral/s
het **katoen** cotton
de **keel** throat; de **~pijn** sore t-
de **keerzijde** back *sheet of paper etc*
kennen to know *(person; ik ken);* **kennis maken** to make acquaintance
het **kentekennummer** registration number
de **kerk** *-en* church/es
de **kerrie** curry
Kerst|avond Christmas Eve; **1e & 2e ~dag** 25 & 26 Dec.; **Vrolijk ~feest** Happy C-
de **ketjapsaus** ketchup
de **ketting** *-en* chain/s
de **keuken** kitchen; cooking/cuisine; de **~handdoek** tea towel

de **keuze** -*n* option/s; **naar ~** choice of
de **kiespijn** toothache
ik **kijk maar rond** I'm just looking; **kijk eens!** have a look! (**kijken** look)
het **kilo** *kilo's* kilo/s; de **~meter** -*s* k-metre/s
het **kind** -*eren* child/ren
het **kinderlbedje** child's bed; het **~menu** c- menu; de **~porties** c- portions
de **kip** *kippen* chicken/s
klaar ready, finished
de **klacht** -*en* complaint/s (**klagen** complain)
klein/e small; **een ~ beetje** a little bit; het **~geld** s- change
de **klep** *kleppen* valve/s
kleren clothes
de **kleur** -*en* colour/s
de **klier** -*en* gland/s
de **klok** *klokken* clock/s
de **klompen** clogs
het **klooster** monastery, nunnery
het **klopt niet** it's wrong *bill*
de **knie** *knieën* knee/s
de **knop** *knoppen* button/s
de **koek** -*en* cake/s; het **koekje** -*s* biscuit/s, cookie/s
de **koelkast** refrigerator
de **koffer** -*s* suitcase/s
de **koffie** -*s* coffee/s; **~ met melk** with milk; **~ met room** with cream; **~ verkeerd** mostly milk; de **~pot** c-pot; de **decafé** decaffeinated c-
de **koffietafel** light lunch of cooked meat, cheese, bread, pastries
ik **kom** I come; **komt aan** arrives; **komt u binnen!** c- in! (**komen** come)
het **kommetje** -*s* bowl/s
de **koning** king; **~in** queen; **Koninginnedag** 30 April; **koninklijk** royal
kontant betalen to pay cash
te **koop** for sale; de **~avond** late shopping night; **~jes** bargains (**kopen** buy)
de **koorts** termperature, fever
het **kopje** -*s* cup/s
de **koplamp** -*en* headlight/s
kort short; te too
de **korting** discount
kosten to cost; de **~** the costs; **dat kost** it costs
koud/e cold
de **kraan** *kranen* tap/s, faucet/s
de **krant** -*en* newspaper/s
de **kredietkaart** -*en* credit card/s
krijgen to get, have
de **kroeg** -*en* bar/s, pub/s
kruiden herbs; **~boter** herb butter

de **kruidenier** grocer
het **kruispunt** crossroads
we **kunnen** we can; **u kunt** you can (**kunnen** be able)
de **kunst** art; de **~galerij** art gallery
de **kurkentrekker** corkscrew
de **kussensloop** -*slopen* pillowcase/s
de **kust** coast
de **kwitantie** -*s* receipt/s
ik **ben... kwijt** I've lost...; **...de weg kwijt** I'm lost (**kwit zijn** be/have lost)

L

laag/lage low; **lage druk** low pressure
de **laan** *lanen* avenue/s
laat late; **later** later; **laatst/e** last
laat mc gerust! leave me alone!
het **laken** -*s* sheet/s; de **~zak** sheet bag
de **lamp** -*en* lamp/s
de **(land)kaart** -*en* map/s; *over* of
lang/lange long, tall; **langer** longer
langs along; **~komen** to come along
langzaam slow; **langzamer** slower
... **laten typen** to have... typed
het **lawaai** noise
leeg empty
leggen to put *(ik leg)*
lekt leaks (**lekken** leak)
de **lekke band** -*en* puncture/s
lekker nice, delicious
lenen to borrow
de **lente** spring
de **lepel** -*s* spoon/s
de **leraar** *leraren* teacher/s
let op! take care!
leuk/e nice
de **leunstoel** -*en* armchair/s
de **leveringsdatum** delivery date
lezen to read, reading
het **lichaam** body
licht light; **~blauw** l- blue
het **licht** -*en* light/s; **ontsteek uw lichten** use headlights
de **lidkaart** membership card
het **lied** *liederen* song/s
het **liefst; liever** preferably
liggen to lie, be situated (**het ligt** it lies)
ik **lijd aan** I have, suffer from (**lijden** suffer)
de **lijn** -*en* line/s
de **lijst** -*en* list/s
links left; **~af** to the left
de **lokale munteenheid** local currency
het **loket** ticket office
de **long** -*en* lung/s
de **loodgieter** plumber
ik **loop** I walk (**lopen** walk)
is **los gekomen** has come off

de **lucht** air; de ~**filter** air filter; de
~**haven** airport
de **lucifer** -s match/es
luid loud
de **luier** -s nappy -pies, diaper/s
het **luik** -en shutter/s

M

de **maag** stomach
de **maagpijn** stomach ache
ik **maak** I make (**maken** make)
maal per dag times per day
de **maaltijd** -en meal/s
de **maand** -en month/s; de ~**stonden**
woman's periods; ~**verbanden**
sanitary towels/napkins
maandag Monday, **ma.** Mon.
maar but; just
maart March
de **maat** maten size/s
de **machine** -s machine/s
de **machinist** -en engineer/s
mag ik may I/may I have (mogen be
allowed)
mager/e thin; skimmed
de **magnetron** microwave
de **makelaar** -laren estate agent/s
maken to make; **afspraak** ~ m- an
appointment
de **man** mannen man/men; husband
marineblauw navy blue
de **markt** -en market/s; de ~**plaats**/het
~**plein** m- place
m.a.w. - met andere woorden in other
words
me me
mee|brengen bring with you, etc;
~**gaan** go with
meenemen take-away, to take with
you etc
het **meel** flour
het **meer** meren lake/s
meest/e most
mei May
het **meisje** -s girl/s
de **melk** milk; **magere** ~ skimmed;
halfvolle ~ semi-skimmed
men one ('you', 'people')
meneer Mr, sir
de **menukaart**, het **menu** menu
de **mensen** people
het **merk** make, brand
het **mes** messen knife/knives
met with; ~ **andere woorden** in other
words
de **meubelen** furniture
mevrouw Mrs/Ms
de **middag** afternoon; **'s middags** in the a-
middelmatig/e moderate

mij/me me
mijn/m'n my; **mijnheer/meneer** Mr, sir
het **mineraalwater** mineral water
de **minuut** minuten minute/s
misschien perhaps
het **mist** it's foggy
moe tired; **ik ben** ~ I'm t-
de **moeder** -s mother/s
moeilijk difficult
de **moer** -en nut/s (metal); de ~**sleutel**
spanner
ik **moet** I must (**moeten** have to)
mogelijk possible, **zo spoedig** ~ as
soon as p-
de **molen** -s mill/s
de **mond** -en mouth/s
de **monteur** mechanic
mooi/e nice, fine, lovely thing
morgen tomorrow; de ~ morning;
morgenochtend tomorrow m-; **'s
morgens** in the m-
de **mosterd** mustard
de **motor** motoren engine, motor/s; de
~**boot** m- boat; de ~**fiets** m-cycle
de **mug** muggen mosquito/es
het **museum** museums/musea museum/s
de **muts** -en woolly hat/s
de **muur** muren wall/s
de **muziek** music

N

na after; ~ **maaltijd** a- meals
de **naald** -en needle/s
de **naam** namen name/s
naar to; **waar** ~ **toe** where to
naast next to
de **nacht** -en night/s; **'s nachts** at n-
de **nagel** -s nail/s
nakijken to check
nat/natte wet
natuurlijk of course
Nederland Netherlands; **Nederlands**
Dutch; **Neder|lander/landse**
person m/f
nee no
ik **neem** I take/I'll have; **neemt u maar**
help yourself (**nemen** take)
net just
het **netnummer** telephone zone number
netto net; ~ **prijs** price before tax
de **neus** nose
niemand no one
niet not; ~ **op** not on; ~ **waar** isn't
it/aren't you etc
niets nothing; ~ **te danken** you're
welcome
nieuw/e new; **nieuwe lijn** n- line
nodig necessary; **ik heb**... **nodig** I
need...

nog some more; still; ~ **een** another one; ~ **niet** not yet; ~ **wat** a little more

de **nooduitgang** emergency exit

nooit never

noord north; de **Noordzee** North Sea

november November

nu now

het **nummer** -s number/s

nuttig useful

O

o.a. - *onder andere* amongst others

of or; whether, if

een **ogenblikje** just a moment

oktober October

de **olie** oil; de ~**filter** o- filter; het ~**peil** o-level

om at; about; **om te** in order to

omdat because

de **omgeving** surrounding area

onbeperkt unlimited *(beperken* to limit)

onder under; de ~**breker punten** *electrical* points

ongetrouwd unmarried

het **ongeval** -*vallen* accident/s

ongeveer approximately

onmiddellijk immediately

onmogelijk impossible

ons/onze us/our; **een ons** 'ounce' 100g

het **ontbijt** breakfast; ~**en** have b-; de ~**granen** b- cereal

ontmoeten to meet

het **ontsmettingsmiddel** antiseptic cream

ontsteek uw lichten switch on your headlights

ontvangen to receive s.t., s.o.

onze our *(see* ons)

het **oog** *ogen* eye/s

ook also; ~ **op** also on; ~ **niet** not either

de **oom** -s uncle/s

het **oor** *oren* ear/s; de ~**pijn** e-ache

oost east

op on; in; **opstaan** to get up

opbellen to phone

open open; on; ~**ingstijden** o-ing hours

opgediend served

de **opinie** opinion; **in mijn** ~ in my o-

opmerken to notice

oproepen to call, summon; **laatste oproep** last call

opschrijven to write down

oranje orange *colour*

oud/e old; de **ouders** parents; **ouderwets** old fashioned

over over; about; via; past *time;* **overal** everywhere

overgeven to vomit

het **overhemd** -*en* shirt/s

het **overige** the rest, remainder; elsewhere

de **overnachting** overnight stay

overstappen to change *trains etc*

P

het **paar** pair, couple; **een** ~ a few

het **paard** -*en* horse/s; ~**rijden** to ride

paars purple

Paasdag Easter Day; **2e/tweede** ~ E-Monday

het **pad** -*en* path/s

de **pakking** -*en* gasket/s

het **paleis** *paleizen* palace/s

de **pannenkoek** -*en* pancake/s

het **papier** paper

de **paraplu** *paraplu's* umbrella/s

het **park** -*en* park/s

de **parkeer**|**automaat**/**meter** parking meter, de ~**garage** multi-storey car park; ~**gelegenheid** p-facilities; de ~**plaats/terrein** car park; de ~**schijf** p- disc

parkeren to park; ~ **verboden** no p-ing

pas op! look out!

Pasen Easter

het **paspoort** passport

de **passagier** -s passenger/s

passend appropriate

het **past** it fits; ~ **niet** it doesn't... (**passen** fit, suit)

patat chips/fries

de **pen** *pennen* pen/s

de **penicilline** penicillin

per se necessarily; **niet per se** not n-

de **persoon** *personen* person/s

photocopiëren to photocopy

de **pijn** -*en* pain; **het doet** ~ it hurts

de **pijp** -*en* pipe/s

Pinksterdag Whit. Sunday; **2e** ~ Whit. Monday

de **plaats** -*en* place/s, seat/s, room; **in** ~ **van** instead of

het **plafond** ceiling

het **plakband** sticky tape

plat still *not fizzy;* flat *land*

het **platteland** countryside

het **plein** *town* square

de **pleister** -s plaster/s, Band-Aid

het **poffertje** -s fritter/s

de **polder** -s polder, reclaimed land

de **polikliniek** outpatients' department

de **politie** police; het ~**bureau** p- station

de **pomp** -*en* pump/s

het **pond** 'pound' 500g

de	portefeuille wallet
de	postbus P.O. box
het	postkantoor post office; hoofd~ main P.O.
de	postzegel -s stamp/s
het	potlood potloden pencil/s
	prachtig wonderful
	praktisch practical
	precies exact/ly
de	prentbriefkaart -en postcard/s
het	pretpark amusement park
	prettig pleasant, nice; ~e reis! have a good trip!
de	prijs prijzen price/s; de ~opgave quotation
	prima excellent, great!
het	probleem -lemen problem/s
	procent per cent
het	product -en product/s; het ~enprogramma p- range
de	productie|capaciteit production capacity; de ~lijn p- line
het	profijt -en profit/s
	proost! cheers!
de	PTT post office (B)
het	publiciteitsmateriaal publicity material

R

het	raam ramen window/s
	rechts right; ~af to the r-; rechtdoor straight on
	regelen to adjust
	regelmatig regularly
de	regen rain; de ~jas raincoat; de ~pijp drainpipe; het regent it's raining
de	regering -en government/s
het	registratiekantoor port (office) of registry
de	reis reizen journey/s; het ~bureau travel agent; de ~cheque traveller's cheque; de ~ziekte travel sickness; prettige ~ have a good trip!
	reizen to travel, go
de	rekening bill/check; bank account; het ~suittreksel -s statement/s
de	rem remmen brake/s; het ~licht b-light; ~blokken b- blocks
	repareren to repair, mend
	reserveren to book, reserve
de	restauratie buffet, restaurant
	retour return ticket
de	richting -en direction/s
het	rijbewijs driving licence
u	rijdt te snel slow down (rijden drive, ride)
	rijk rich;
	rijks- national; ~weg main road
de	rivier -en river/s

	roepen to call
de	rok rokken skirt/s
	rokers smokers, niet~~ non-smokers (roken smoke)
de	rolstoel -en wheelchair/s; ~faciliteiten w- facilities
de	rondleiding -en guided tour/s
de	rondrit -ritten tour/s
het	rondpunt -en roundabout/s
de	rondvaart -en round trip; cruise; de ~boot pleasure boat
	rood/rode red; rare meat
de	room cream
	roze pink
de	rug back
de	rugzak rucksack
dit	ruikt this smells (ruiken smell)
de	ruitenwissers windscreen wipers
op	rust retired; rustig quiet
	ruw/e rough

S

	samen (al)together
de	sceptische put septic tank
het	schaafwondje graze
de	schaal schalen dish/es
de	schaar pair of scissors
de	schaats -en skate/s; ~en to skate, skating
de	schakelaar light switch
de	schatting -en estimate/s
	scheepsonderdelen boat spares
het	scheerapparaat shaver; de ~crème shaving cream; het ~mes razor
	schelen: het kan niet ~ never mind
het	schijnt dat it seems that (schijnen seem)
	schikt u dat is that convenient for you (schikken be convenient)
de	schilder decorator
het	schilderij -en painting/s
het	schip schepen ship/s
de	schoen -en shoe/s; size de maat
de	schokdemper -s shock absorber/s
de	school scholen school/s
	schoon clean (~maken to clean)
de	schoorsteen -stenen chimney/s
het	schotel -s saucer/s
de	schouder -s shoulder/s
	schrijven to write (ik schrijf); schriftelijk in writing
de	schroef schroeven screw/s; de schroevendraaier s- driver
het	seizoen -en season/s
de	senior -en pensioner/s
	september September
u	serveert you serve (serveren serve)
de	short pair of shorts
de	sigaret -retten cigarette/s

het s**i**naasappel *-en* orange/s; het ~**sap** o- juice

s**i**nds since

de sj**aa**l *-s* scarf, scarves

de sl**aa**pzetel *-s* reclining chair/s

sl**aa**t **af** is stalling *(afslaan* stall)

de slagboom *-bomen* barrier/s

de slager butcher

de sl**aa**p**|**kamer bedroom; de ~**plaats** couchette; de ~**zak** sleeping bag (**slapen** sleep)

slecht bad; ~ **wegdek** road subsidence

slepen to tow

de sleutel *-s* key/s; (**moer**)**s-** spanner

het slot *-en* lock/s *door*

de sluis *sluizen* lock/s *canal*

sluiten to close *(gesloten* closed)

dit sm**aa**kt that tastes: **lekker** nice, **vies** bad; **het ~ mij niet** I don't like it (**smaken** taste)

sm**a**kelijk! enjoy your meal, bon appétit!

smal/smalle narrow

de sn**ee**uw snow; ~**kettingen** s- chains; het sn**ee**uwt it's snowing

(te) snel (too) fast; de ~**trein** express train

snoep sweets

de soep soup

de sok *sokken* sock/s

soms sometimes; perhaps

soorten sorts of

de spaak *spaken* spoke/s

de specialit**ei**t *-en* speciality -ties

het speelgoed toys; **een stuk ~** a toy

het spel *spellen* game/s; **wat speelt** what's on (**spelen** play)

hoe spel je how do you spell (**spellen** spell)

de spiegel *-s* mirror/s

de spier *-en* muscle/s; de ~**band** ligament

de spijkerbroek jeans

de spijskaart menu

het spijt me I'm sorry

de spin**a**zie spinach

zo sp**oe**dig m**o**gelijk as soon as possible

het spoor *sporen* platform/s; de ~**weg** raillway/road

het sportterr**ei**n sports ground

ik spreek I speak, talk; **u spreekt** you speak (**spreken** speak)

het sp**u**itwater fizzy water

het staal *stalen* sample/s; **bloed/urine ~** blood/urine s-

staan to stand, be

staan... **toe** to allow *(toestaan* allow)

de stad *steden* town/s; het ~**huis** t- hall; het ~**scentrum** t- centre

starten to start

het station *-s* station/s

steek... **over** cross... *(oversteken* cross)

de stekker *-s* plug/s

sterk strong

stil/stille quiet; **stiller** quieter

de stoel *-en* chair/s

de stofzuiger vacuum cleaner

de stomerij dry cleaner's

de stoom**|**boot steamer; de ~**trein/tram** steam train/tram

het stopcontact *-en* socket/s

de stoptrein *-en* local/stopping train/s

de storm *-en* storm/s; de ~**waarschuwing** gale warning

de straat *straten* street/s

het strand *-en* beach/es

het stratenplan street map

het strijkijzer iron *for clothes*

de strippenkaart *-en* ticket strip/s

de stroming *-en* current/s

de student *-en* student/s (**studeren** study)

het stuk *-s* piece/s; **per ~** each

het stuur handlebars

stuurboord starboard

de suiker sugar; de ~**ziekte** diabetes

de supermarkt supermarket

surf**|**en to go surfing, de ~**plank** *-en* surfboard/s

T

't it

de taal *talen* language/s

de taart *-en* large cake/s; tart/s

de tafel *-s* table/s

de tak *takken* branch/es

talentvol clever

de tand**|**arts dentist; de ~**enborstel** toothbrush; de ~**pasta** t-paste

de tante *-n* aunt/s

het tarief *tarieven* tarif, rate/s

de tarwe wheat

de tas *tassen* bag; het **tasje** carrier bag

te too; ~ **koop** for sale

de teen *-en* toe/s

de tegel *-s* tile/s

tegen against; ~**over** opposite

t**e**kenen to sign

de telefoon *-s* telephone/s; het ~**boek** t- directory; de ~**kaart** phonecard; het ~**nummer** t- number

de televisie, **tv** TV; de ~**antenne** TV aerial

tellen to count

tenminste at least

tenn**i**ssen to play tennis; het **tennis** tennis; de **bal,** *ballen* ball/s; het **racket** *-s* racket/s

de tent -en tent/s
de tentoonstelling -en exhibition/s
terug back; ~bellen ring b-; ~betalen pay b-; ~brengen bring b-; geld ~gave refund; ~keren return; ~komen come b-; ~sturen send b-
het theater -s theatre/s
de thee tea; het ~lepeltje t-spoon; de ~pot t-pot
thuis at home; ~komen to come home
tien ten
het tij -en tide/s
de tijd time
de timmerman carpenter
t/m - tot en met from – to – inclusive
t/o - tegenover opposite
de toegang admittance; het ~sbewijs ticket; de ~sprijs fee; vrije ~ a-free
toegestaan permitted
toekennen to award contract, prize
toenemende increasing (toenemen increase)
het toerisme tourism; de toerist -en tourist/s
met toeslag with supplement
toestaan to allow
het toestelnummer extension number
toesturen to send
toets code in enter code
de tomaat tomaten tomato/es
tonen to show
de toren -s tower/s
tot to, until; ~ aan as far as; ~ uw dienst you're welcome; ~ ziens see you again
het totaal total
het touw -en, touwtje -s rope/s
de tram -s tram/s; de ~halte t- stop
de trap stairs
de trein -en train/s; de ~taxi t- taxi; met de ~ gaan go by t-
de trui -en sweater/s
het T-shirt -s T-shirt/s
de tuin -en garden/s, yard/s
de tulp -en tulip/s
de tunnel -s tunnel/s
tussen between
twee two; ~de second; ~maal twice
de tweepersoonskamer double room
de tweesprong crossroads

U

u you polite; u. o'clock, hour abbr.
de ui -en, het uitje -s onion/s
uit out; from country
de uitgang exit; gate airport

uitgezonderd except
de uitlaat exhaust
de uitrit exit; ~ vrachtwagens lorry e-
uitsluitend exclusively, only
uitstekend excellent
de uitverkoop bargains, sale
de uitvoer export
uitwendig gebruik external use
de uitwijkplaats layby
de universiteit -en university -ties
het uur uren, u. o'clock, hour
uw your

V

v.a. -vanaf from, since
hoe vaak how often
de vaatwasmachine dishwasher
de vader -s father/s
de vakantie holiday/s, vacation; ik ben met ~ I'm on h-
de vakken marked spaces parking
de vallei -en valley/s
van of; from
vanlavond this evening; ~daag today; ~morgen this morning; ~nacht tonight; waar ~daan where from
vanuit from
vat: van het ~ draught beer
veel much, many, a lot of; hoe ~ how m-; te ~ too m-
de vegetariër -s vegetarian/s person; vegetarisch/e v- food
veilig safe from danger
het venster -s window/s
ver far
veranderen to change
de verantwoordelijke person in charge
het verband -en bandage/s; connection/s
verblijven to stay, reside
verboden prohibited; ~ te roken no smoking; ~ toegang no admittance
de verdeler distributor goods
verder nog iets would you like anything else
de verdieping -en storey/s, floor/s; beneden~ ground f-
de Verenigde Staten/V.S. the United States
de vergadering -en meeting/s
vergeten to forget; ik ben het ~ I've forgotten
de vergissing -en mistake/s
de vergunning permit; ~ houders p-holders
de verjaardag -en birthday/s; Gelukkige V-! Happy B-!
het verkeer traffic; de ~slichten t- lights
verkeerd wrong; dat is ~ that's w-
verklaren to explain

de **verkoop** sales; **verkoopt u** do you sell (**verkopen** sell)
de **verlichting** light
vers/e fresh
het **verschil** difference; **verschillend**/e different
verschuldigd: hoeveel ben ik ~ what do I owe you
de **versnelling** gears, de ~**sbak** gearbox; de ~**spook** clutch
verstaan to understand, know (ik **versta**)
verstandig sensible, intelligent
versturen to send
vertalen to translate
ik **vertegenwoordig** I represent; de ~**er** representative
het **vertrek** -*trekken* departure/s (**vertrekken** depart)
verwachten to expect
de **verwarming** heating
de **verzekering** insurance, **omnium** ~ comprehensive i-
op **verzoek** on request
vet fat, fatty
vier four
vies dirty
vijf five
vinden to find; like; think: **vind je** (**niet**) do (don't) you think so
de **vinger** -*s* finger/s
de **vis** fish; de ~**boer** f-monger (**vissen** fish)
het **Vlaams**/e Flemish; **Vlaanderen** Flanders
het **vlees** meat
het **vliegtuig** -*en* plane/s
de **vloer** -*en* floor/s
de **vlucht** -*en* flight/s, het ~**nummer** f-number
vlug quick/ly
de **voet** -*en* foot/feet; ~**ballen** play football; de ~**balmatch** f-ball match; het ~**pad** f-path
voetgangers pedestrians; het ~**gebied** pedestrian precinct
de **vogel** -*s* bird/s
vol full; ~**geboekt** fully booked
volg! follow; **volgend**/e next (**volgen** follow)
voltanken to fill up
de **volwassene** -*n* adult/s
voor for, before, in front (of); het ~**beeld** example; ~**gerechten** appetisers; **op** ~**hand** in advance; de ~**kant** front *side;* bij ~**keur** preferably; de ~**naam** first name; ~**rang geven** give way; het ~**schot** deposit; het ~**schrift** -*en*

prescription/s
voorstellen to introduce, suggest; de **voorstelling** performance
de **voortent** -*en* awning/s
de **voorruit** windscreen, windshield
voorzichtig careful; ~ **rijden** drive carefully
de **vork** -*en* fork/s
vragen to ask
de **vriend** -en friend/s, **vriendin** -**dinnen** f; **vriendelijk** friendly
de **vrieskast** freezer
vrij free, available, vacant; rather
vrijdag Friday; **vr.** Fri.
vroeg early
ik **vroeg** I asked for (**vragen** ask)
de **vrouw** -*en* woman/women; wife
de **vrucht** -*en* fruit
de **V.S.** -*Verenigde Staten* United States
de **V-snaar** fan belt
het **vuilnis** rubbish, trash; de ~**bak** r-bin/t- can; het ~**blik** dustpan; de ~**omhaling** r- collection
de **VVV** tourist office *(NL)*

W

het **waait** it's windy
waar where; **waarin** in which
waar true; **dat is** ~ that's true
waarom why
wachten to wait; ~ **op** w- for; ~ **eens** w- a minute!
de **wachtkamer** waiting room
de **wagen** car
de **wandeling** -*en* walk/s
wanneer when
warm hot
de **wasmachine** washing machine
wassen to wash
de **wastafel** washbasin
wat what; some; ~ **van** some of that; how; ~ **voor** w- kind of
waterskiën water skiing, to go w- s-
de **watten** cottonwool
we we
weer again
het **weer** weather; de ~**svoorspelling** weather forecast
ik/u **weet** I/you know (**weten** know)
ga **weg!** go away!
de **weg** -*en* road/s
wegens because of
wegslepen to tow away
weinig not much, few; **een** ~ a little
welk/e which
het **werk** work; ~**dagen** weekdays; ~**loos** unemployed
werken to work *(ik werk)* ...**werkt** (**niet**) ... (doesn't) work

de **wesp** -*en* wasp/s
weten to know, know how to *(ik weet)*
wie who; **van ~** whose
het **wiel** -*en* wheel/s
de **wielrijder** -*s* cyclist/s
wij/we we
de **wijk** -*en* district/s
de **wijn** -*en* wine/s
ik **wil** I want; **wilt u** do you w- (**willen** want)
de **wind** wind; **~surfen** windsurfing, to go w-
de **windmolen** -*s* windmill/s
de **winkel** -*s* shop/s
de **winter** winter
wisselen to change; het **wisselkantoor** exchange bureau
wit/witte white
woensdag Wednesday, **wo**. Wed.
de **wol** wool
woon/woont live/s (**wonen** live)
de **woon**lkamer living room; de **~plaats** home town
het **woord** -*en* word/s; het **~enboek** dictionary
wordt is, becomes (**worden** be, become)
het **woud** forest, wood

Z

de **zaak** matter, business; cause (**zaken doen** do business)
zacht soft
de **zak** *zakken* pocket/s
de **zakdoek** -*en* handkerchief -chieves; **papieren ~jes** paper h-
de **zaklantaarn** torch, flashlight
zal shall, will
het **zand** sand
zaterdag Saturday, **za**. Sat.
ze them
de **zee** sea; **ruwe/kalme ~** rough/calm s-; **~vruchten** seafood

de **zeep** soap; het **~poeder** s- powder
zeer very
zeggen to say, tell; **zegt u het maar** what would you like
zeker certain/ly, sure
de **zekering** -*en* fuse/s
zelfde same
de **zenuw** -*en* nerve/s
ziek ill
het **zieken**lhuis hospital; de **~wagen** ambulance
zien to see; **hoe ziet het eruit** what does it look like
zij/ze she, they
zijn to be, are
zijn/z'e his, its
zilverkleurig silver *colour*
zingen to sing *(ik zing)*
het **zit vast** it's stuck; **gaat u zitten** please sit down (**zitten** sit; fit)
zo, so, like this; **zo'n** *(zo een)* one of those/like that
ik **zoek** I'm looking for (**zoeken** look for)
de **zomer** summer
de **zon** sun
zondag Sunday; **zo**. Sun.
zonder without; **~ datum** undated
de **zonne**lbrand sunburn; de **~bril** sunglasses; de **~crème** suntan cream; **zonnig** sunny
de **zoon** -*s* son/s
het **zout** salt
zuid south
we **zullen** we shall
de **zus** *zussen*, **zuster** -*s* sister/s
zwaar heavy
zwanger pregnant
zwart/e black; **zwarte bessen** blackcurrants
zwemlmen to swim; het **~bad** s- pool; de **~broek** trunks; de **~gordel** lifebelt; het **~pak** costume; het **~vest** lifejacket

A

a/an een 22,96

be **able** kunnen 97; **I can** ik kan; **you can** u kunt

about over 45,88; *approximately* ongeveer

above boven

abroad het buitenland

accident/s het ongeval -*vallen* 81

actual/ly eigenlijk

adder/s de adder -s 82

address het adres *adressen* 61,93

to **adjust** regelen 72

admittance de toegang 88; ~ **fee** de t-sprijs; ~ **free** vrije t-gang; **no** ~ verboden t-; ~ **ticket** het t-sbewijs

adult/s de volwassene -*n* 7

in **advance** op voorhand 63

after na 84

afternoon de middag; **good** ~ goede-8,94; **in the** ~ 's middags 59

again weer

against tegen 46

age 7,83,89

ago geleden

air de lucht 72; ~ **filter** de l-filter 70; ~**port** de l-haven 54,80

all *everything* alles; **that's** ~ dat is alles 39; ~ **day** de gehele dag; *whole* heel

allergic allergisch, *to* voor 84

to **allow** toestaan 63 (staan... toe); *permitted* toegestaan 68

almost bijna

alone: leave me ~ laat me gerust 93

along langs

alphabet het alfabet 54

already al 82

also ook 20; ~ **on** ook op 75

altogether samen 39

always altijd

I **am** ik ben 84 *(to be* zijn 97)

ambulance de ziekenwagen 81

America Amerika, de V.S 52,92; **American** Amerikaans

amongst others o.a. - *onder andere*

amount het bedrag; ~**s to** bedraagt 7,63 (**to** ~ **to** bedragen)

and en 9

animal/s het dier -*en*

ankle/s de enkel -s 85

another een ander 9; ~ **one** graag een

answer het antwoord (**to** ~ antwoorden)

antifreeze de anti-vries 72

antiseptic cream het ontsmettingsmiddel 47

anything else iets anders; **would you like** ~ verder nog iets 38

apartment/s het appartement -*en*

appendix de blindedarm 85

apple/s de appel -*s* 30,38; ~ **juice** het appelsap

to **apply to** gelden; **does not** ~ **to** geldt niet voor 68

appointment/s de afspraak -*spraken* 58; **make an** ~ a- maken 59,84

approximately ongeveer

apricots abrikozen 43

April april 95

are zijn 20 *(to be* zijn 97); **there is/are** er is/zijn 17,97

area/s het gebied -*en*

arm de arm -*en* 85

around om; *approximately* ongeveer

to **arrive** aankomen; ~**d** aangekomen 80; **arrival** de aankomst 75,80

art de kunst; ~ **gallery** de kunstgalerij

artichoke/s de artisjok -*sjokken* 42

as als; ~ **on** als op 75

to **ask** vragen 57; **I** ~**ed for** ik vroeg 28; *requested* gevraagd 63

asparagus de asperges 42

aspirin de aspirine 47

assembly *machine* de assemblage 62

asthma astma 84

at aan 50; *time* om 58; *from* bij 51

attacked aangevallen 93 (**to attack** aanvallen)

aubergines aubergines 42

August augustus 95

aunt/s de tante -n

Australia Australië 92; ~**n** Australiër/Australisch *m/f*

autumn de herfst 95

available vrij (21),24,57,59,90

avocado/s de avocado *avocado's* 42

to **award** *contract* toekennen 63

awning/s de voortent -*en* 7

B

baby de baby; ~ **food** de b-voeding 47

back terug 57,73,91; *of person* de rug 85; *of page* de keerzijde

bad slecht; *food* vies 28

bag de tas *tassen* 93; *carrier* ~ het tasje; *luggage* 74,80

baggage locker/s de bagagekluis -*kluizen* 74

baker de bakker 39
ball/s de bal *ballen;* **foot~** de voetbal 87
banana/s de banaan *bananen* 43
bandage/s het verband -*en* 47
Band-Aid de pleister -*s* 47
bank/s de bank -*en* 51; ~ **account** de rekening 63; ~ **card** de b-kaart 63; ~ **statement** het rekeningsuittreksel 63
bar/s de kroeg -*en* (23)
barrier/s de slagboom -*bomen* 21
batch, ~ **of** *(production)* de groep (producten) 62
bath het bad 10, ~**room** de b-kamer 17
battery -ries de batterij -*en* 45; *car* 70
to **be** zijn 97 (ik ben 84); *become* worden 21; *situated* liggen
to **be able** kunnen 97; *(I can* ik kan)
beach/es het strand -*en* 64
beans bonen 31; *runner* boontjes 31,42
beautiful mooi
because omdat; ~ **of** wegens
to **become** worden; *(is, will be)* wordt 21
bed/s het bed *bedden* 10,21; ~**room** de slaapkamer 10,16; **child's ~** kinderb- 10
bee/s de bij -*en*
beef het rundvlees 30,35,40
been: I have ~ ik ben + past participle (ge...) 82,97
beer het bier 23; **draught ~** b- van het vat
beetroot de rode biet 42
before voor 84
to **begin** beginnen 87; ~**ning** het begin
behind achter 68
Belgium België 3,90; **Belgian** Belg/Belgische *m/f* 92
to **belong** behoren; **who does... ~ to** aan wie behoort...
below beneden
belt/s de broeksriem -*en* 48
bend/s de bocht -*en;* **dangerous ~** gevaarlijke b-
bent gebogen 72 (**to bend** buigen)
better, best beter, best (12)
between tussen
bicycle/s de fiets -*en* 67,69; **by ~** op de   ; **c- path** het f-pad 69; **cyclists** f-ers; *hire* 69; *parts* 70-71 (**to ~** fietsen)
big groot 29,49
bill/s de rekening -*en; hotel* 13; *restaurant* 22,28; *shop* 39,50
bird/s de vogel -*s*

birthday/s de verjaardag -*en;* **Happy B-** Gelukkige Verjaardag
biscuit/s het koekje -*s* 44
a **bit more/less** wat meer/minder 38
bite/s de beet *beten* 46; **bitten by a...** door een... gebeten 82 (**to ~** bijten)
black zwart fc; ~**berries** braambessen 43; ~**currants** zwarte bessen 29; ~ **pudding** de bloedworst 40
blanket/ s de deken -*s* 14,16
blocked geblokkeerd 15 (**to block** blokkeren)
blood het bloed; **high ~ pressure** hoge b-druk 84; ~ **sample** het b-staal 83
blouse/s de blouse -*es* 48
blue blauw 49,fc; ~**berries** bosbessen 43; **dark/light ~** donker/lichtb- fc, **navy ~** marineb-fc
to **board, boarding** instappen 80
boat/s de boot *boten* 78-79; **pleasure ~** rondvaartb-; *parts* scheepsonderdelen 79
body het lichaam 85
boiler de boiler 17
bon appétit! smakelijk! 22
bone/s het bot *botten* 85
book/s het boek -*en* 45,96; ~**shop** de b-handel
to **book** reserveren 7,26; ~**ed** gereserveerd 8; ~**ing** de boeking 80; *camping* 7,20; *entertainment* 87; *hotel* 7,8-11; *meal* 26; *travel* 76-78
to **borrow** lenen 14
both beide
bottle/s de fles *flessen* 20; het **flesje** 29; ~ **opener** de flessenopener 45
bowels de darmen 85
bowl/s het kommetje -*s* 19
boy/s de jongen -*s* 92
brake/s de rem *remmen* 72, ~ **light** het r-licht 72, ~ **blocks** r-blokken 72
branch/es de tak *takken* 62
bread het brood 25,39; *roll*/s het broodje -*s* 22,23,39
to **break** breken; **broken** gebroken 15; kapot
breakdown 69; **broken down** defect 69
breakfast het ontbijt 13,25; ~ **cereal** o-granen 44; **to have ~** o-en
bridge/s de brug *bruggen* 64; **over the ~** de b- over
briefs: *ladies'* de damesslip 48; *men's* de herenslip 48

to **bring** brengen; ~ **back** terugb- 73; ~
   with *you etc.* meeb-
broken gebroken 15; kapot
brother/s de broer -s 89
brown bruin fc; ~ **café** het bruin café
   22
brush/es de borstel -s 19
buffet de restauratie 75
to **build** bouwen; ~**er** de aannemer 15;
   ~**ing**/s het gebouw -en
bulb/s *light* de gloeilamp -en 16,70
bus/es de bus *bussen* 77; ~ **station**
   het b-station 77; ~ **stop** de b-
   halte 77
business het bedrijf 56-63; **to do** ~
   zaken doen 59
I'm **busy** ik heb het druk (**to be** ~ druk
   hebben)
but maar
butcher de slager 40
butter de boter 25,44
button de knop *knoppen* 68
to **buy** kopen (45)
by: **car** per auto; ~ **bicycle** per fiets;
   ~ **boat** per schip; ~ **train** met de
   trein

C

cabbage de kool 42; **red** ~ rode kool
   35
cabin/s de cabine -s 78
cable/s de kabel -s 70
café het café, eetcafé 22
cake/s de koek -en, de taart -en; ~
   shop de banketbakker 39
to **call** roepen; **be called** heten 24,89;
   ring bellen 57,81
calm kalm 79
camera het fototoestel
camping 7,20-21; ~ **carnet** het
   kampeercarnet; ~**site** de camping
   20; *Gaz* 20; *pitch* de kampplaats
I **can** ik kan 7,25,132; **we** ~ we
   kunnen 25; **you** ~ u kunt 50; **I**
   can't ik kan niet; *may I* mag ik 8
   (be able kunnen 97)
can/s het blik *blikken;* ~ **opener** de
   blikopener 45
Canada Canada 92; **Canadian**
   Canadees
canal/s *wide* het kanaal -*nalen* 78;
   narrow de gracht -en 64
to **cancel** annuleren
capital city de hoofdstad
car/s de auto *auto's* 67; **by** ~ met de
   auto; ~ **hire** auto verhuur 73; ~
   park de parkeerplaats 8,68;
   parts 70-71
caravan/s de caravan -s 7,20; **motor**
   ~ de kampeerauto 7,20

card: **post**~ de prentbriefkaart 45;
   visiting ~ het kaartje 58
care: **take** ~! let op! 67; ~**ful**
   voorzichtig; **drive** ~**fully**
   voorzichtig rijden
carpenter de timmerman 15
carrot/s de wortel -en 42
in **case** indien 84
cashl **desk** de kassa 50,51; ~
   dispenser de geldautomaat 51;
   cashier de kassier 51; **pay** ~
   kontant betalen 51
castle/s het kasteel -*stelen* 64,88
cat/s de kat *katten*
cathedral/s de kathedraal -*dralen* 64
cauliflower de bloemkool 42
celery de selder 42
ceiling het plafond 16
central heating de centrale
   verwarming 17
centre het centrum; **town** ~
   stadscentrum 65
cereal *breakfast* de ontbijtgranen 44
certain/ly (ja)zeker 9,58
chain de ketting 70; **snow** ~**s**
   sneeuwkettingen 71
chair/s de stoel -en 19; **arm**~ de
   leunstoel 16; **reclining** ~ de
   slaapzetel 78
chandlery *boat parts*
   scheepsonderdelen 79
to **change** veranderen 80; *bus etc.*
   overstappen 75,76; *goods*
   wisselen 50; *money* 51
the **Channel** het Kanaal; **C- Tunnel** de
   Kanaaltunnel
chapel/s de kapel -*pellen*
in **charge**: **person in** ~ de
   verantwoordelijke 56
cheap goedkoop; ~**er** goedkoper 12
check/bill de rekening; *hotel* 13;
   restaurant 22,28; *shop* 39,50
to **check** nakijken 72; ~ **in** inchecken
   80
cheers! proost! 22
cheese de kaas 23,33,44
chemist de apotheek 46-47
cheque/s de cheque -s 63
cherries kersen, krieken 43
chest de borst 85
chicken/s de kip *kippen* 33,40
chicory het witlof 42
child/ren het kind -*deren*
   7,20,88,89,92
child'sl **bed** het kinderlbedje 10; ~
   menu het k-menu; ~ **portions** k-
   porties 28
chimney/s de schoorsteen -*stenen*
   14
chips *Br* frites, patat 23; *Am* chips

chocolate de chocolade; **hot** ~ de warme c-melk 25; ~ **ice cream** het c-ijsje 29

choice/s de keus *keuzen* 68,74; ~ **of** naar keuze 34,63

chop/s de karbonade -*n* 40

Christmas Kerstlmis; ~ **Day** eerste K-dag 75; ~ **Eve** K-avond; **Happy** ~ Vrolijk K-feest 95

church/es de kerk -*en* 64

cigarette/s de sigaret -*retten* 45

cinema de bioscoop 64,87; *what's on* wat speelt 87

clean schoon (**to** ~ schoonmaken)

clever talentvol; *intelligent* verstandig

o' **clock**: **at**...~ om...uur 59; *time* 21,26,**55**

clogs de klompen

closed gesloten 21,38,79; *turned off* dicht 17 (**to** ~ sluiten)

closet/s de kast -*en* 16

clothes kleren 48-49

clutch de versnellingspook 70

coast/s de kust -*en*

coat/s de jas *jassen* 48

cod de kabeljauw 41

area **code** *phone* het netnummer

coffee/s de koffie -*s* 23,25; ~ **pot** de k-pot 19; **decaffeinated** ~ de decafé 23

cola cola; **diet** ~ c- light 23

cold koud 17; **a** ~ een verkoudheid; **I'm/it's** ~ 95

colleague/s de collega *collega's* 60

to **collect** afhalen 51

colour/s de kleur -*en* 49,fc

comb/s de kam *kammen* 47

to **come** komen 59,90 (ik kom); ~ **along** langsk- 90; ~ **back** terugk- 91; ~ **home** thuisk-; ~ **in!** komt u binnen!; **has** ~ **off** is los gekomen 15

commission de commissie 63

company -nies de firma *firma's* 57; **subsidiary** ~ het dochterbedrijf 62

complaint/s de klacht -*en; **make a** ~ een k- indienen 50 (**complain** klagen)

complicated ingewikkeld

component/s de component -*en* 62

computer de computer 61; ~ **disk** de diskette 61; ~ **programme** c-programma 61

concert/s het concert -*en* 87

condom/s het condoom -*domen* 47

congratulations on... proficiat met... *('profissee-at')*

connection *travel* het verband; *piece* de aansluiting 20

constipation constipatie 46

contents de inhoud 93

contract/s het contract -*en* 63

be **convenient** schikken; **is that** ~ **for you** schikt u dat 59

to **cook** bakken 28; ~**er** het fornuis 18; ~**ing** de keuken; *well-done* doorgebakken 27

cookie/s het koekje -*s* 44

copy copies het exemplaar -*plaren*

corkscrew de kurkentrekker 45

corner/s de hoek -*en* 66

it **costs** dat kost 21,38,132; **the** ~ de kosten 63; **to cost** kosten 15

cot het kinderbed 10

cotton het katoen; ~**wool** de watten 47; *thread* het garen 45

couchette de slaapplaats 76

to **cough, coughing** hoesten 46

to **count** rekenen, tellen

countries 90; *from* uit 92

countryside het platteland

courgettes courgettes 42

of **course** natuurlijk 12

crab/s de krab *krabben* 41

cracked gebarsten 15 (**to crack** barsten)

crayfish kreeftjes 33, rivierkreeftjes 35

cream: *food* de room 35; *skin* de crème 47

credit card/s de kredietkaart -*en* 50

crisps *Br* chips

croissant/s de croissant -*s*

cross... steek...over 66 (**to** ~ oversteken)

crossroads het kruispunt 66

cucumber de komkommer 42

cup/s het kopje -*s* 19

cupboard/s de kast -*en* 16

currants bessen 43; **black**~ zwarte b- 29

currency: **local** ~ de lokale munteenheid 63

current/s de stroming -*en* 79

curtain/s het gordijn -*en* 16; ~ **rail** de g-stang 16

customs de douane; ~ **officer** de d-beambte 79

cutlery 19,22

to **cycle** fietsen (ik fiets); ~ **hire** 69,71; ~ **path** het fietspad; **cyclist/s** de wielrijder -*s*

D

daily dagelijks

to **dance, dancing** dansen 91

danger het gevaar 78; ~**ous** gevaarlijk

dark donker; ~ **blue** d-blauw fc

date 59,80; **delivery** ~ de leveringsdatum *-s* 63; *stamping tickets* 75;
undated zonder datum 74
daughter/s de dochter *-s* 89,92
day/s de dag *-en* (9),73;
68,87,94; **all** ~ de gehele dag
dear *price* duur 12; ~**er** duurder 49;
too ~ te duur 49
Dear Sir or Madam Geachte Heer,
Mevrouw 7
December december 95
deck het dek
to **decide** besluiten; **decided** besloten
declare: anything to ~ iets aan te
geven
decorator de behanger, de schilder
15
decreasing afnemend 79
delicatessen fijne en bereide
vleeswaren 40
delicious lekker 27; heerlijk 91
delighted prettig 60,89
delivery date de leveringsdatum 63
dentist de tandarts 84
deodorant de deodorant 47
departure het vertrek 80 (**depart**
vertrekken)
it **depends on**... het hangt af van...
deposit het voorschot 7
dessert het dessert 27
detergent het afwasproduct 44
diabetes de suikerziekte 84
diaper/s de luier *-s* 47
diarrhoea de diaree 46
dictionary het woordenboek 45
diesel de diesel 72
difference het verschil; **different**
verschillend
difficult moeilijk
dike/s de dijk *-en*
dining room de eetkamer
dinner *evening* het avondmaal/diner
13,22
direct direct 80
direction/s de richting *-en* 74,75;
locations 66
director de direkteur 56
dirty vies 28
disabled andersvaliden 7
disco de disco 87
discount de korting 63,88
dish/es de schaal *schalen* (19);
menu het gerecht *-en* 28
dishwasher de vaatwasmachine 18
disk/s de diskette *-n* 61
distributor *goods* de verdeler 62
district/s de wijk *-en*
divorced gescheiden
to **do** doen 15,93; **I** ~ ik doe, **you** ~ u
doet 28

doctor/s de dokter *-s* 81-84
dog/s de hond *-en* 82
dollar/s de dollar *-s* 50,51
door/s de deur *-en* 14
double room de tweepersoonskamer
7,8,10
down neer; ~**stairs** beneden
drain/s de goot *goten* 14; ~**pipe** de
regenpijp 14
how **dreadful** hoe erg
dress/es de jurk *-en* 48
dressing *bandage* de verband 47
drink/s het drankje *-s; soft* ~ de fris,
frisdranken 23,91; **to** ~ drinken
29,**91**; *alcoholic* de borrel 90;
non-alc. alcoholvrij
to **drip** druipen
to **drive** rijden 67; **driving licence** het
rijbewijs 73
drugstore de apotheek, de drogist
46-47
dry droog; ~ **cleaner's** de stomerij
duck/s de eend *-en* 31,40
during, *for* gedurende 84
dustbin de vuilnisbak (18)
dustpan het vuilnisblik 19
Dutch Nederlands 45,132; *person m/f*
Nederllander/landse 92
duvet het dekbed 16

E

each elk/e 88,96; ~ **one** per stuk 38;
~ **other** elkaar 90
ear/s het oor *oren* 85; ~**ache** de
oorpijn 46
early vroeg
east oost 64
Easter Pasen 95; ~ **Day** Paasdag; ~
Monday Tweede/2e Paasdag 75
easy gemakkelijk
to **eat** eten 83
eel/s de paling *-en* 30,34,41
egg/s het ei *eieren* 25,31,44
eggplants aubergines 42
eiderdown het dekbed 16
eight acht 26,131; **eighty** tachtig
131
not **either** ook niet
elbow/s de elleboog *-bogen* 85
elecltric elektrisch; ~**trics** *car* het
elektrische systeem 70; ~**trician**
de elektricien 15; ~**tricity** de
elektriciteit 17,20; *fuse box* de
elektriciteitskast 17
else: **would you like anything** ~
verder nog iets 38
email het email 61
embassy de ambassade
emergency 46,69,81; ~ **exit** de
nooduitgang; *phone nos.* 53,81

empty leeg 17
end het einde
engaged *occupied* bezet 56,66
engine de motor 70; **engineer/s** de
  machinist -*en* 79
English *thing* Engels 45,92,132;
  person m/f Engelsman/Engelse;
  ~-**speaking** Engelstalig 88;
  England Engeland 52,92
enjoy your meal smakelijk 22
enough genoeg
enter code toets code in 74
entertainment 87
entrance/s de ingang -*en* 77;
  admittance de toegang 88; ~ **fee**
  de toegangsprijs; ~ **free** vrije
  toegang 88; ~ **ticket** het
  toegangsbewijs
no **entry** geen toegang
envelope/s de enveloppe -*n*
epilepsy de epilepsie 84
escalope/s *veal* het (kalfs)lapje -*s* 40
especially vooral
estate agent/s de makelaar -*laren*
estimate de schatting 63
etc. enz. *(enzovoort)*
Europe Europa
evening/s de avond -*en;* **good** ~
  goedenavond 94; **this** ~
  vanavond 8,90; **in the** ~ 's
  avonds 94; ~ **meal** het
  avondmaal 13,22
every elk 88; ~...**hours** elke...uur 84
every|**one** iedereen; ~**thing** alles 39;
  ~**where** overal
exact/ly precies
example het voorbeeld; **for** ~ b.v. *(bij
  voorbeeld)*
excellent prima, uitstekend
except uitgezonderd 67; behalve
exchange: **bureau** het wisselkantoor
  51; **to** ~ **goods** wisselen 50
excluded niet inbegrepen (13)
exclusive exclusief 13; *only*
  uitsluitend 68
excuse me pardon 14,132
exhibition/s de tentoonstelling -*en* 88
exhaust de uitlaat 70
exit de uitgang 74; **emergency** ~ de
  noodu-; **motorway** ~ de afrit 67
to **expect** verwachten
expensive duur 12,49; **too** ~ te d-
to **explain** verklaren
export de uitvoer 56; **to** ~ **goods**
  goederen uitvoeren
express| **train** de sneltrein 75; ~**way**
  de autosnelweg 67
extension number het toestelnummer
  56
external use uitwendig gebruik

extra extra 14
eye/s het oog *de ogen* 85

F
face het gezicht
facilities faciliteiten
factory -ries de fabriek *fabrieken*
fall *season* de herfst 95
family -lies de familie -*s* 92; ~ **room**
  de familiekamer 10
famous beroemd
fan belt de V-snaar 70
far ver; **as** ~ **as** tot aan 66; **how** ~
  hoe ver 66
farm/s de boerderij -*en*
fast snel, hard; **too** ~ te snel 67; ~
  food 22,23
fat dik; *food* vet
father/s de vader -*s* 92
faucet/s de kraan *kranen* 17
favourite favoriet
fax de fax 61
February februari 95
I'm **fed up** ik ben (het) beu
fence/s de afsluiting -*en* 14
ferry de ferry 78
festival het festival -*s* 52
fever de koorts 82
a **few** enkele, een paar; *not many* weinig
figs vijgen 43
fill it up voltanken 72
film/s de film -*s* (85); *camera* het f-
  rolletje 45; *slides* voor dia's 45
filter de filter *cigarettes* 45; **air/oil** ~
  de luchtfilter/oliefilter 70
finally eindelijk
finance 63
to **find** vinden 45,79; ~ **a seat** 24; *like*
  90; *the way* 66
fine goed 9,89; ~ **thanks** g- dank u
  132; *great!* prima!
finger/s de vinger -*s* 85
it **finishes** het eindigt (**to** ~ eindigen)
finished klaar; ~ **products**
  eindproducten 62
fire: *brigade* de brandweer 53,81;
  ~**place** de haard 16
firm *company* het bedrijf, het firma
  57,58,62
first eerst 12,59,66
First Aid post eerste hulppost
fish de vis 27,41; ~**monger** de
  visboer 41; **to** ~, ~**ing** vissen 86;
  permit de vergunning 86
it **fits** het past; **it doesn't** ~ het past
  niet 49 (**to** ~ passen)
five vijf 131; **fifth** vijfde 59
Flanders Vlaanderen; **Flemish** het
  Vlaams
flashlight de zaklantaarn 45

flat/s *apartment* de flat -*s; tire* de lekke band 71; *land* plat

flight/s de vlucht -*en* 80; ~ **number** het v-nummer 80

floor/s de vloer -*en* 16; *storey* de verdieping 12,59; ~**cloth** de dweil 19; **ground** ~ de benedenverdieping 7,12

flour het meel

flower/s de bloem -*en*

it's **foggy** het mist 95

to **follow** volgen; **follow!** volg! 67

I'm **fond of...** ik hou veel van...

food het eten

foot/feet de voet -*en* 85; ~**ball match** de v-balmatch 87; **play ~ball** v-ballen; ~**path** het voetpad

for voor 8,52; *during* gedurende 84; *since* al 82

forbidden verboden

foreign buitenlands 80; ~**er**/s buitenlander -*s*

forest het bos, het woud 65

to **forget** vergeten; **I've forgotten (it)** ik ben (het) vergeten

fork/s de vork -*en* 19,22

form/s het formulier -*en* 93

a **fortnight** veertien dagen

four vier 131; **fourth** vierde 59

France Frankrijk 92; **French** Frans/e *m/f*

free *available* vrij (21),24,57,59,90; *cost* gratis 88; *WC* vrij 66

freezer de vrieskast 18

fresh vers

Friday vrijdag 68,94; *(dates)* 59

fridge de ijskast 18, de koelkast

fried gebakken (**to ~** bakken)

friend/s de vriend -*en,* vriendin -*dinnen (f)* 89,90; ~**ly** vriendelijk, gezellig

fries frites, patat 23

fritter/s het poffertje -*s* 22

from van 13; *country* uit 92; **where** ~ waar vandaan 92; **from – to – incl.** t/m *(tot en met)* 68

in **front (of)** voor 66; ~ (**side**) de voorkant

fruit de vrucht, het fruit 43; ~ **juice** het fruitsap 23,44

frying pan de braadpan 19

fuel *petrol* de benzine 72,79; *gas, electricity* 17

full vol 68; ~ **up** v-geboekt 9; **fill it up** v-tanken 72

furniture de meubelen

fuse/s de zekering -*en* 17,70

G

gale warning de stormwaarschuwing 79

game/s het spel *spellen* 86; *food* wild 37,40; *match* 87

garage/s de garage -*s* 69

garden/s de tuin -*en* 14

garlic het knoflook 42

gas het gas 17; ~ **bottle** de g-fles 17,20; ~ **station** het benzine-station 72; *fuel* de benzine 72; *pilot light* het g-lichtje 17

gasket/s de pakking -*en* 70

gate *airport* de uitgang 80

gears de versnelling 70; **gearbox** de v-sbak 70

genuine echt

German Duits/e *m/f* 92, **Germany** Duitsland 92

to **get** *find* vinden 45,79; *have* krijgen; ~ **off** afstappen 77; ~ **up** opstaan; **how do I ~ to** hoe ga ik naar 66,77

girl/s het meisje -*s* 92; ~**friend** de vriendin 89

to **give** geven 24,56 (ik geef); ~ **way** voorrang geven; *pass s.t. on* doorgeven

gland/s de klier -*en* 85

glass/es het glas *glazen* 22,23,91

glasses *spectacles* de bril

gloves handschoenen 48

glow plug/s de kaars -*en,* de bougie -*s* 71

gluten-free gluten-vrij

to **go** gaan (ik ga) 77,87,**97**; ~ **away!** ga weg! 93; ~ **with** *you etc* meegaan; *depart* vertrekken 76

golden goudkleurig fc

golf: **to play ~** golfen 86; ~ **club**/s de golfclub -*s* 86

good goed 11,38,96; ~ **day** g-endag 21; ~ **evening** g-enavond 9; ~ **morning** g-emorgen 8; ~ **night** g-enacht 94

goodbye dag, tot ziens 13,91,132

gooseberries kruisbessen 43

government/s de regering -*en*

gram/s het gram *grammen* 38

grand|**father**/**mother** de groot|vader/moeder 92

grapefruit de pompelmoes -*moezen* 43

grapes druiven 43

grateful dankbaar 61

graze het schaafwondje 46

great! prima!

Great Britain Groot-Brittanië 52,92

green groen fc; ~ **card** de groene kaart

greetings 94,132

grey grijs fc

grilled gegrild 32 (**to grill** grillen)

grocer de kruidenier 44
ground de grond; ~ **floor** de benedenverdieping 7,12
group/s de groep -en; batch of (production) 62
guide/s de gids -en 88; ~**d tour** de rondleiding

H

had: **I/we** ~ ik had/we hadden 91,97 (hebben); **I** ~ **to** ik moest 97 (moeten)
haddock de schelvis 41
hair het haar; ~**dresser** de kapper; *barber* herenkapper; ~ **dryer** de h-droger 18
half half 38; ~ **past** half 55; **one and a** ~ anderh- 131
ham de ham 23,32,40
hamburger de hamburger
hammer de hamer
hand/s de hand -en 85; ~**bag** de tas 93
handkerchief -ieves de zakdoek -en 48; **paper** ~ het papieren zakdoekje 47
handlebars het stuur 70
happened: **what's** ~ wat is gebeurd
happy gelukkig 95
harbour/s de haven -s 78; ~ **master** de havenmeester 79
hard hard; *difficult* moeilijk
hat/s de hoed -en 48; **woolly** ~ de muts 48
to **have** hebben 97; **I** ~ ik heb 8; **we** ~ we hebben 23; ~ **you** heeft u 26; ~ **to** moeten 97; *suffer from* lijden aan 84; *I'll take* ik neem 27,59
hay fever de hooikoorts 44
he hij/ie 14,57,97
head het hoofd 85; ~**ache** de h-pijn 46; ~ **office** het h-bureau 62
headlight/s de koplamp -en 70; **use** ~**s** ontsteek uw lichten 67
to **hear** horen (ik hoor)
heart het hart 84,85
heating de verwarming; **central** ~ de centrale v- 17
heavy zwaar
hello dag 8,132; *phone* hallo 53
helmet/s de helm -en
help! help! 81; **can I** ~ **you** kan ik u h-en 49; **can you** ~ **me** kunt u me h-en 93; ~ **yourself** neemt u maar 91; **thanks for your** ~ dank for uw hulp 14 (**to** ~ helpen)
her haar 56,57,97
here hier 50,66; ~ **you are** alsjeblieft 38,39; **not** ~ 57

herring/s de haring -en 22,32,41
high hoog
hill/s de heuvel -s, de berg -en 64
him hem 57
hip/s de heup -en 85
to **hire** huren 73,86; **for** ~ te huur 71
his zijn 56,57,97
hobby -bies de hobby *hobby's* 91
hold: **please** ~ blijf aan de lijn 56
hole/s het gat -en
holiday/s de vakantie; **I'm on** ~ ik ben met v-; **public** ~**s** publieke feestdagen 52,75
Holland Nederland 90,92
go **home** naar huis gaan; **at** ~ thuis; **come** ~ thuiskomen; ~ **made** eigengemaakt 31; ~ **town** de woonplaats
honey de honing 44
to **hope** hopen 59; **I** ~ **so** dat hoop ik; **I** ~ **not** dat hoop ik niet
horse/s het paard -en; ~ **riding** paardrijden 86
hospital het ziekenhuis 81
hostel/s *youth* de jeugdherberg -en 21; ~ **manager** de huisbewaarder 21
hot warm 17,25,95; **very** ~ heet
hotel/s het hotel -s 7,8-13
hour/s het uur *uren* 21,26,**55**,59; h. *abbr.* 68
house/s het huis *huizen* 14,96; **at your** ~**/place** bij u 7
how hoe 77; ~ **are you** h- gaat het 89,132; ~ **long** h- lang 15,73,90; ~ **many** h-veel 9,20; ~ **much is it** h-veel kost dat 38,72,86,132; ~ **do I get to** hoe ga ik naar 66, hoe kom ik bij 77
I'm **hungry** ik heb honger 22 (**be** ~ honger hebben)
hurry: **I'm in a** ~ ik heb haast
my - **hurts** mijn... doet pijn 82,84,85
my **husband** mijn man 89

I

I ik 7,97
ice het ijs; ~ **blocks** ijsblokken 79; ~ **cream**/s het ijsje -s 29,33; **with** ~ met ijs 23
idea/s het idee *ideeën*
identity card/s de identiteitskaart -en 8
if als
ill ziek 82; *illness* 81-85
immediately onmiddellijk
to **import** importeren
important belangrijk
impossible onmogelijk
in in 90,95

included inbegrepen 17,73; inclusief
13,63; **not** ~ exclusief 13
inclusive: **from**... **to**... **incl**. t/m *(tot
en met)* 68
to **increase** toenemen; ~**ing**
toenemende 79
Indonesian food 37
industry de industrie, het bedrijf;
industrial area het
industrieterrein
infected geïnfecteerd (**infect**
infecteren)
information de informatie; *about* over
62,88; inlichtingen 74
inland binnenland 75,80
inner tube/s de binnenband *-en* 71
insect: **bite**/s de insecten|beet *-beten*
46; ~ **repellant** het i-verwerend
middel 47
inside binnen; *contents* de inhoud 93
instead of i.p.v. *(in plaats van)*
insulin de insuline (84)
insurance de verzekering 73;
comprehensive ~ omnium v-
interest *rate* de interest 63
I'm **interested in** ik interesseer me voor
(**be** ~ zich interesseren)
interesting interessant
international buitenlands 80;
internationaal 75
internet het internet
to **introduce** voorstellen 60,89
invitations 90
invoice/s de factuur *facturen* 63 (**to**
~ factureren 63)
Ireland Ierland 92; **Irish** Iers/e *m/f* 92
iron *for clothes* het strijkijzer 18
is is 13,132 *(to be* zijn 97); **isn't it?**
etc niet waar; **there is/are** er
is/zijn 17; *be situated* liggen
island/s het eiland *-en* 64
it het, 't 55; **its** zijn 97

J

jacket/s het jasje *-n*
jam de jam 25,44
January januari 95
jeans de jeans 48, de spijkerbroek 48
job/s het baantje *-s*, de baan *banen*
joint *body* de gewricht
journey/s de reis *reizen* 78; **have a
good** ~ prettige reis! 67
jug/s de kan *kannen* 19
juice het fruitsap 23,44
July juli 95
June juni 95
just net 59; ~ **a moment** een
ogenblikje 26,53; ~ **as** even
8,49; ~ **looking** 38; *only* slechts,
maar 91

K

kebabs shoarma 22
key/s de sleutel *-s* 11,14; **ignition** ~
contactsleutel 71
kilo/s het kilo *kilo's* 38,62; ~**metre**/s
de kilometer *-s* 73
kind: **what** ~ **of** wat voor 23,73
king de koning; *royal* koninklijk
kipper de bokking 41
kitchen de keuken 18-19
knee/s de knie *knieën* 85
knickers de damesslip 48
knife/knives het mes *messen* 19,22
to **know** *s.t.* weten; **I** ~ ik weet; **I don't** ~
ik weet het niet 132; **you** ~ u
weet 56; *person* kennen; **well-
known** bekend; *make
acquaintance* kennis maken 89

L

ladder de ladder 14
ladies' dames; ~ **briefs** de damesslip
48; *toilets* de WC
lake/s het meer *meren* 64
lamb *meat* het lamsvlees
27,30,33,40
lamp/s de lamp *-en* 16
language/s de taal *talen*
large groot 49
last laatst 76,80; **to** ~ duren 15,78
late laat; **later** later 15,57
lavatory de WC 10,17,24,66
lay-by de uitwijkplaats
to **leak** lekken; **leaks** lekt 15,17
at **least** tenminste
to **leave** vertrekken 90; ~ **behind**
achterlaten 57,73; ~ **me alone!**
laat me gerust! 93
leek/s de prei *-en*, het look 42
left links; **to the** ~ linksaf 66; ~
luggage 74
leg/s het been *benen* 85
lemon/s de citroen *-en* 23,43
less minder 38
letter/s de brief *brieven* 61
lettuce de sla 42
library de bibliotheek
to **lie** *be situated* liggen (**it lies** het ligt)
life|belt de zwemgordel 78; ~**jacket**
het zwemvest 78
lift de lift 12,59
ligament de spierband 85
light licht; ~ **blue** l-blauw fc
light/s het licht *-en*, de verlichting 16,
de lamp *-en* 71; ~ **bulb**/s de
gloeilamp *-en* 16,70; ~ **switch** de
schakelaar 17
lighter de aansteker 45
I'd **like** mag ik 22,56,132; graag 42; *I
want* ik wil, wil graag 62; *enjoy* ik

hou van 91; *food* 27,91: **I don't ~
it** ik vind het niet leuk; *place*
vinden 90
like this zo 29,39
line/s de lijn *-en* 56,78; **new ~**
nieuwe l- 62; **production ~** de
productielijn 62
list/s de lijst *-en* 62
to **listen to** horen (ik hoor)
little klein; **a ~** een beetje 90, een
weinig; **a ~ more** nog wat 91,
wat meer 38
to **live** wonen 14,90 (ik woon); **living
room** de woonkamer 16
liver de lever 40
lobster de kreeft 41
locations 66
lock/s *canal* de sluis sluizen 79; *door*
het slot *-en* 14; **luggage ~ers**
bagagekluizen 74 (**to ~**
opsluiten)
long lang 9,78; ~**er** langer 28; **a ~
time** een lange tijd
to **look** kijken; **look!** kijk eens!; ~ **at**
kijken naar; ~ **for** zoeken 14,49; I
~ **forward to** ik verheug me op;
just ~ing ik kijk maar rond 38;
what does it ~ like hoe ziet het
er uit? 93; **it ~s (bad)** het ziet er
(slecht) uit
lorry -ries de vrachtwagen *-s*
I've **lost** ik ben... kwijt 93,132; **I'm ~** ik
ben de weg kwijt 132 (**to lose**
kwit zijn)
lost property gevonden/verloren
voorwerpen
a **lot**, ~ **of** veel
loud luid
lovely leuk, heerlijk 91
low laag
LPG *fuel* het autogas 72
luggage de bagage 80; ~ **carrier** het
b-rek 71; ~ **lockers** b-kluizen
74; ~ **strap** de b-riem 71
lunch de lunch 13,22; *light, cold* de
koffietafel 22
lung/s de long *-en* 85
Luxembourg Luxemburg 92;
Luxemburger *m/f* de
Luxemlburger/burgse

M

machine/s de machine *-s* 62, de
automaat *-maten*
mackerel de makreel 41
mail 52
make *brand* het merk 69; **to ~**
maken 84 (ik maak)
man/men de man *mannen;* **men's** -
heren- 48,66

manager/s de directeur *-en* 56;
export/sales ~ d- voor de
uitvoer/verkoop 56
many: how ~ hoeveel 38; **not ~** niet
veel, weinig
map/s de (land)kaart *-en* 45; *of* over;
street ~ het stratenplan 45
March maart 95
margarine de margarine 44
marina de jachthaven 78
market de markt 64; ~ **place** de
marktplaats/het marktplein 64
married getrouwd
match *game* het spel 86
match/es de lucifer *-s* 45
material/s de stof *stoffen;* **raw ~s**
grondstoffen 62
matter: what's the ~ wat is er aan de
hand 81; **it doesn't ~** het geeft
niet 132
May mei 95
may I, ~ have mag ik 22,47,56,132
(be allowed mogen)
me me 15,50; **for ~** voor me 61
meal/s de maaltijd *-en* 13,22;
before/after ~s voor/na de
maaltijd 84; **enjoy your ~**
smakelijk! 22; ~*times* 22;
ordering 27
mean: what does that ~ wat betekent
dat (**to ~** betekenen)
meat het vlees 27,30,40; *rare* rood
27; *well-done* doorgebakken 27
mechanic de monteur (79)
medicine het geneesmiddel 47, 83,
84
medium medium 73
to **meet** ontmoeten 90; **nice to ~ you**
prettig met u kennis te maken
60,91
meeting/s de vergadering *-en* 57
melon/s de meloen *-en* 43
membership card de lidkaart 21
to **mend** repareren 15,72
mention: don't ~ it niets te danken;
tot uw dienst 57.132
menu het menu, de menukaart 22,27;
30-37
message de boodschap 57
meter de meter 17
metro de metro 78
microwave de magnetron 18
milk de melk 25,44; ~**shake**
milkshake 23; **semi-skimmed ~**
halfvolle m- 44; **skimmed ~**
magere m- 44
mill/s de molen *-s*
minced meat het gehakt 40
mind: never ~ het kan niet schelen
mine *of me* van mij

mineral water het mineraalwater 29;
fizzy het spuitwater 29; *not fizzy*
plat 29
minute/s de minuut *minuten* 55; **just
a ~** een ogenblikje 26,53
mirror/s de spiegel -*s* 17
to miss missen; **missed** gemist 74
mistake/s de vergissing -*en* 74; *bill*
28
mobile phone de GSM 57
moderate middelmatig 79
moment het ogenblik 26; **just a ~**
een ogenblikje 26,53
monastery, nunnery het klooster
Monday maandag 59,68,80,92
money het geld 51, 63; *cash
dispenser* de geldautomaat 51;
refund geld teruggave 68; *small
change* het kleingeld 51
month/s de maand -*en* 95
moped de bromfiets 67,(69)
more meer 38; **a little ~** nog wat 91;
no ~ geen 17
morning/s de morgen -*s;* **good ~**
goede- 8,94; **in the ~** 's morgens
59,84; **this ~** vanm-
mosquito/es de mug *muggen*
most meest
mother/s de moeder -*s* 92
motor/s de motor -*en* 70; **~boat** de
m-boot; **~ caravan** de
kampeerauto 7,20; **~cycle** de m-
fiets 67; **~way** de
autoweg/snelweg 67; *parts* 70-71
mouth/s de mond -*en* 85
movie/s de film -*s*; **~ theater** de
bioscoop 64,87; *what's on* wat
speelt 87
Mr de heer, meneer 7,12,56,58,61
Mrs/Ms mevrouw 56,58,61
much veel; **how ~ is it** hoev- kost dat
38,132; **not ~** niet v-, weinig; **too
~** te v- 12
mug/s de beker -*s* 19
muscle/s de spier -*en* 85
museum/s het museum
museums/musea 64,88
mushroom/s de champignon -*s* 42
music de muziek (87),91
mussels mosselen 41
I must ik moet 73,93 *(have to* moeten
97)
mustard de mosterd 34,44
my mijn/m'n 92,93,97

N

nail/s de nagel -*s*
name/s de naam *namen* 26,89; **first
~** de voornaam 93
nappy -pies de luier -*s* 47; **~ cream**

de crème voor de billetjes 47
narrow smal
nationality 92
navy blue marineblauw fc
near dichtbij; **~by** in de buurt 9,38;
~est dichtstbijzijnde 69
nearly bijna
(not) necessarily (niet) per se 61
neck de hals 85
I need... ik heb...nodig 70,81;
it doesn't ~ het hoeft niet 61
(**to ~** be/hoeven)
needle/s de naald -*en* 45
nerve/s de zenuw -*en* 85
net *price* netto; *before tax* netto prijs
63
the Netherlands Nederland 90,92
never nooit; **~ mind** het kan niet
schelen
new nieuw 62
New Zealand Nieuw-Zeeland 92;
person m/f Nieuw-
Zeelander/landse
newspaper/s de krant -*en* 45
next volgend 76,80; *n- to* naast 66
nice leuk 90,(91), aardig; mooi
night/s de nacht -*en* 9,21; **at ~** 's
nachts 94; **good ~** goeden- 94;
to~ vanavond
no nee 97,132; **~ one** niemand;
none geen 17,93,96
noise het lawaai 12
non-alcoholic alcoholvrij
north noord 64; **N- Sea** de Noordzee
nose de neus 85
not niet 49,57,97; **~ at all** niets te
danken 57; **~ either** ook niet;
~ on niet op 75
nothing niets; **~ else** niets anders
to notice opmerken
November november 95
now nu 15,57,69
number/s het nummer -*s* 53,56,131;
registration ~ het
kentekennummer 8
nut/s de noot *noten* 28,34,43; *metal*
de moer -*en* 71
nutmeg de muskaatnoot

O

occupied bezet 56,66; *unoccupied,
free* vrij 24
October oktober 95
of van 57; **~ course** natuurlijk 12
offer: special ~ de aanbieding 49
off: turned ~ dicht 17
office/s het kantoor -*toren* 56,59;
tourist ~ de VVV, het bureau
voor toerisme 88
how often hoe vaak 77

oil de olie 44; ~ **filter** de o-filter 70; ~
   level het o-peil 72
OK goed, OK 15,132
old oud 83,89; *retired* op rust 90
omelette/s de omelet *-letten* 31,34
on op 75, aan; *switch* open 17;
   what's ~ *cinema* wat speelt 87
once eenmaal
one een 22; ~ **and a half** anderhalf
   131; ~-**way traffic** e-
   richtingsverkeer; *'you'* men
onion/s de ui *uien* 42
only alleen 74; ~ **on** alleen op 75;
   pedestrians ~ alleen voor
   voetgangers; *exclusively*
   uitsluitend 68
open open 38,79, geopend 88; ~**ing**
   hours openingstijden 38 (**to** ~
   openen)
opinion: **in my** ~ in mijn opinie
opposite tegenover 66
option/s de keus *keuzen* 68,74;
   choice of naar keuze 34,63
or of 29
orange/s het sinaasappel *-en* 43; ~
   juice het sinaasappelsap 23;
   colour oranje fc
order de bestelling; ~ **form** de b-
   snota 63; **out of** ~ buiten gebruik;
   place an ~ b- plaatsen 63; **to** ~
   bestellen 63; **I** ~**ed** ik bestelde 28
ordinary gewoon
other ander 9,12; **each** ~ elkaar 90
our ons/onze 58,63,97
out *he/she is not in* 57
out uit 67
outboard motor de buitenboordmotor
   78
outpatients' department de
   polikliniek 81
outside buiten
over over; ~ **there** ginds 51
overnight stay de overnachting
owe: **what do I** ~ **you** hoeveel ben ik
   verschuldigd 83
own eigen
oysters oesters 41

P

page/s de bladzijde *-n*
pain/s de pijn *-en* 46,84,85; **in case**
   of ~ indien u p- heeft 84
painting/s het schilderij *-en*
pair het paar
palace/s het paleis *paleizen* 64
pan/s *saucepan* de pan *pannen* 18;
   frying ~ de braadp- 19
pancake/s de pannenkoek *-en* 22
paper het papier 44
paracetamol de paracetamol

pardon pardon 20,132
parents de ouders 92
park/s het park *-en* 64; *amusement*
   het pretpark
to **park** parkeren 8,68; *car* ~ de
   parkeerlplaats/terrein 68; *multi-*
   storey de p-garage 68
parkingl **disc** de parkeerlschijf 68; ~
   facilities p-gelegenheid; ~ **meter**
   de p-automaat/meter 68; **no** ~
   parkeren verboden; *marked*
   spaces vakken 68
part/s het deel *delen* 70-71,79
party -ties het feest *-en*
to **pass on** *message etc* doorgeven
passenger/s de passagier *-s* 80
passport/s het paspoort *-en* 8,93
past *time* over, *to* voor 55
pasta de pasta 44
paté de paté 31,40
path/s het pad *-en*
to **pay** betalen 13,24,28,50; ~ **back**
   terugb- 50
peach/es de perzik *-en* 43
peanut/s pinda's 34; ~ **butter**
   pindakaas 34
pear/s de peer *peren* 43
pea/s erwten 23,42; ~ **soup**
   erwtensoep 31
pedestrians voetgangers; ~ **only**
   alleen voor v-; **precinct** het v-
   gebied
pen/s de pen *pennen* 45; **pencil** het
   potlood 45
penicillin de penicilline 84
pensioner/s de gepensioneerde -n,
   de a.o.w. 88, de senior *-en*;
   retired aan de a.o.w. *(NL)* 88, op
   rust *(B)* 90
people de mensen, het volk; *'people'*
   say men zegt
pepper de peper 44;
   red/green/yellow ~
   rode/groene/gele p- 42
per per; ~ **cent** procent 63; ~ **day** p-
   dag 73,86; ~ **year** p- jaar 63
perfect perfect 49
performance/s de voorstelling *-en* 87
perhaps misschien, soms
periods *woman's* maandstonden
   (47)
to **permit** toestaan 63 (staan... toe); ~
   holders vergunning houders 68;
   ~**ted** toegestaan 68
person/s de persoon *personen* 9,56;
   ~ **responsible** de
   verantwoordelijke 56
pests *people* 93
petrol de benzine 72; ~ **station** het
   b-station 72

pharmacy de apotheek 46
to **phone** bellen 54; **I ~** ik bel 57
photo/s de foto *foto's* (45)
to **photocopy** photocopiëren 61
picture/s het schilderij *-en*
piece/s het stuk *-s* 38
pike de snoek 41
pillow/s het hoofdkussen *-s* 16;
~**case/s** de kussensloop *-slopen*
16
pilot light het gaslichtje 17
pineapple/s de ananas *-nassen* 43
pink roze fc
pipe/s de pijp *-en* 14,17
pistachio pistachio 29
pizza/s de pizza *pizza's* 40
place/s de plaats *-en; bed* 21;
campsite 20
plaice de schol 41
plan *town* het stratenplan 45,64-65
plane/s het vliegtuig *-en* 80
plaster/s de pleister *-s* 47
plate/s het bord *-en* 19
platform/s het spoor *sporen* 74,76
to **play** spelen; ~ **golf** golfen, ~ **tennis**
tennissen 86
pleasant gezellig; ~**ries** 60,89
please alsjeblieft 8,38,132; graag
39,132; *formal* alstublieft
pleased to meet you prettig met u
kennis te maken 60,89,91
plug/s *electric* de stekker *-s* 17
plumber de loodgieter 15; *plumbing*
17
plum/s de pruim *-en* 43
PO box de postbus
pocket/s de zak *zakken*
points *car electrics* de onderbreker
punten 71
polder/s de polder *-s*
police de politie 81; ~ **station** het p-
bureau 93
pop concert het popconcert 87
pork het varkensvlees 30,40
port de haven; *side* bakboord 78; ~
of registry het registratiekantoor
79
possible mogelijk; **as soon as** ~ zo
spoedig m- 84
post|box de brievenbus; ~**card/s** de
prentbriefkaart *-en* 45; *(main)* PO
het (hoofd)postkantoor 52, de
PTT
potato/es de aardappel *-en* 30,42
practical praktisch
prawns garnalen 41
I **prefer** ik neem liever; ~**ably** bij
voorkeur 59
pregnant zwanger 84
prescription/s het voorschrift *-en* 83

present/s het cadeau *-s,* kado *-s*
(to) **press** (in)drukken 74,77
pressure *tyre* de banddruk 71;
high/low ~ hoge/lage d- 79
pretty mooi
price/s de prijs *prijzen* 62,63,87,132;
inclusive ~ 63; ~ **list** de p-lijst
62; **purchase** ~ de aankoopsom
50; *quotation* de prijsopgave 63
priority *road* 67,69
problem/s het probleem *-lemen*
15,28; *flights* 80; *theft, loss* 93
product/s het product *-en* 62; ~
range het productenprogramma
62
production| capacity de productie-
capaciteit 62; ~ **line** de
productielijn 62
profit/s het profijt *-en*
pro forma pro-forma 63; ~ **invoice**
de p-f- factuur 63
programme *computer* het
programma 61
prohibited verboden
projector/s de projector *-s* 61
pub/s de kroeg *-en* (22,23)
public holidays publieke feestdagen
52,75
publicity material het
publiciteitsmateriaal 62
pump/s de pomp *-en* 71
puncture de lekke band 71; ~ **repair
kit** de reparatiekit 71
purple paars fc
to **push** duwen
to **put** leggen (ik leg)

Q

quantities 38
quay de kade
queen de koningin; ~**'s birthday**
Koninginnedag (30 April) 75
queries *bills* 28
questions 97
quiche de quiche 40
quick/ly vlug 81,91
quieter stiller 12; **quiet** stil, rustig
quotation *price* de prijsopgave 63

R

rabbit/s het konijn *-en* 40
radiator de radiator 71
radio/s de radio *radio's*
radishes radijsjes 42
rail|way/road de spoorweg 74-76
rain de regen; ~**coat** de regenjas 48;
it's ~ing het regent 95
range: **product** ~ het
productenprogramma 62
rare *meat* rood 27

rarely zelden, bijna nooit
raspberries frambozen 43
rate/s het tarief *tarieven* 7,68
rather vrij, nogal; **I'd** ~ **(have)** ik (neem) liever
raw materials grondstoffen 62
razor het scheermes 47
to **read, reading** lezen 91 (ik lees)
ready klaar
real echt
receipt/s het bonnetje -*s* 13,50, de kwitantie -*s* 63
to **receive** ontvangen 61
to **reckon** rekenen
reclining chair/s de slaapzetel -*s* 78
to **recommend** aanbevelen 15, aanraden 88
red rood 29,fc
refrigerator de ijskast 18, de koelkast
to **refund** terugbetalen 50; **a** ~ geld teruggave 68
registration number het kentekennummer 8
registry: port/office of ~ het registratiekantoor 79
regularly regelmatig 83
relations *family* 89,92
I **remember** ik herinner mij; **I can't** ~ ik ben het vergeten
to **rent** huren 73 (ik huur)
to **repair** repareren 15,72
repeat: can you ~ **that** kunt u dat herhalen 132 (**to** ~ herhalen)
reply -lies het antwoord -*en* (**to** ~ antwoorden)
I **represent** ik vertegenwoordig 58; ~**ative** de vertegenwoordiger 62
on **request** op verzoek; ~**ed** gevraagd 63; *requests* 15
reservation de boeking 80; *camping* 7,20; *entertainment* 87; *hotel* 7,8-11; *meal* 26; *travel* 76-78,80
to **reserve** reserveren 7,26; ~**d** gereserveerd 8
responsible person de verantwoordelijke 56
restaurant/s het restaurant -*s* 26-29
retired *(NL)* aan de a.o.w. 88; *(B)* op rust 90; *pensionar* de gepensioneerde
to **return** terugkeren; ~ **ticket to...** heen en terug naar... 76, retour 74; *take back* terugbrengen 73
rhubarb de rabarber 43
rib/s de rib *ribben* 85
rice de rijst 35,44
rich rijk
to **ride, riding** rijden 86
right rechts; **to the** ~ rechtsaf 66;

I'm/you're ~ ik heb/u hebt gelijk; **that's** ~ dat is correct
to **ring** bellen; ~ **back** terugbellen 57
rissoles kroketten 22
river/s de rivier -*en*
road/s de weg -*en* 66; **main** ~ de rijksw-, hoofdstraat; **no through** ~ doodlopende w-; **private** ~ eigen w-; ~ **signs** 67-69
robbery de overval 93
roll/s het broodje -*s* 22,25,39
roof/s het dak -*en* 14,15
room/s de kamer -*s* 8,10; ~**s available** kamers vrij 8; *bed* de plaats 21; *inspecting* 12; *see also* single, double
rope/s het touwtje -*s*, het touw -*en* 45
rough ruw 79
round trip *ticket* heen en terug 76, retour 74
roundabout/s het rondpunt -*en* 66
rubbish het vuilnis 18; ~ **bin** de v-bak; ~ **collection** de v-omhaling 14
rucksack de rugzak

S

safe *from danger* veilig
to **sail, sailing** zeilen 78-79
salad de salade 32
salami de salami 40
sales de verkoop 56; *bargains* koopjes, de uitverkoop 49; **for sale** te koop
salmon de zalm 37,41
salt/y zout 43
the **same** de/het selfde
sample het staal; **blood/urine** ~ bloed/urine s- 83
sand het zand
sandwich *open* de boterham; *roll* het broodje 22
sanitary napkin/s, **towel**/s de maandverband -*en* 47
Saturday zaterdag 68,90,94; *(dates)* 59
saucepan/s de pan *pannen* 18
saucer/s het schotel -*s* 18
sausage/s de worst -*en* 40
to **say** zeggen 77; **what did you** ~ wat zei u 132
scarf/scarves de sjaal -*s* 48
school/s de school *scholen;* **high** ~ het gymnasium *gymnasia*
scissors de schaar 45
scoop/s het bolletje -*s* 29
Scotland Schotland, **Scottish** Schots/e *m/f* 92
screw/s de schroef *schroeven* 71; ~**driver** de schroevendraaier 71

sea de zee 79; **rough/calm** ~ ruwe/kalme zee 79; ~**sickness** de reisziekte 46

seafood zeevruchten 41

season/s het seizoen -*en* 95

seat/s de plaats -*en* 24; de zitplaats -*en* 76

second tweede 59

to **see** zien (ik sie) 12; ~ **you again** tot ziens 13,91; *receive s.o.* ontvangen 61

it **seems that** het schijnt dat (**seem** schijnen)

self|catering 14-19; ~ **service** 24

to **sell** verkopen; **do you** ~ verkoopt u 52

to **send** versturen 61, toesturen 62; ~ **back** terugsturen

September september 95

septic tank de sceptische put 14

serve: **do you** ~ serveert u 13 (**to** ~ serveren)

service| included inclusief bediening 22; ~ **charges** 22,54

shade *out of the sun* uit de zon 7

I **shall/will** ik zal 54; **we** ~ wij zullen 90

shampoo de shampoo 47

shaver het scheerlapparaat 17; ~**ing cream** de s-crème 47; ~**ing point** 17

she zij/ze 57,83,97

sheet/s het laken -*s* 16; ~ **bag** de lakenzak 21

ship/s het schip *schepen* 79; *parts* scheepsonderdelen 79

shirt/s het hemd -*en* 48, de T-shirt 48

shock absorber/s de schokdemper -*s* 71

shoe/s de schoen -*en* 48; *size* de maat 86

shop/s de winkel -*s* 38-50

shopping| centre het winkelcentrum; ~ **hours** 38; **late** ~ **night** de koopavond 38,68

short kort (49); **too** ~ te kort; **pair of** ~**s** de short 48

shoulder/s de schouder -*s* 85

to **show** tonen 15

shower/s de douche -*s* 7,10,17

shrimps garnalen 41

shut gesloten 21,38 *(close* sluiten)

shutter/s het luik -*en* 16

be **sick** overgeven 82; **travel** ~**ness** de reisziekte 46

sights de bezienswaardigheden 88

to **sign** tekenen 51

silencer de geluidsdemper 71

silver *colour* zilverkleurig fc

since sinds

to **sing** zingen (ik zing)

single: **room** de eenpersoonkamer 7,8,10; *ticket* enkele reis 74,76; *unmarried* ongetrouwd

sink de gootsteen 18

Sir meneer 12; **Dear S-** Geachte Heer 7

sister/s de zus *zussen*, zuster -*s* 89

to **sit** zitten; **please** ~ **down** gaat u z- 91

be **situated** liggen (**it is** ~ het ligt)

size/s *clothes* de maat *maten* 49; *shoes* 86

to **skate, skating** schaatsen 86; **skates** de schaatsen 86

skin de huid

skirt/s de rok *rokken* 47

to **sleep** slapen; ~**ing bag** de slaapzak 21; *sheet bag* de lakenzak 21

slippery glad; ~ **road** gladde weg

slow/ly langzaam; **more** ~**ly** langzamer 132

small klein 29,38,49

to **smell** ruiken; **this** ~**s** dit ruikt 28

to **smoke** roken 45 (ik rook); (**non**) **smokers** (niet) rokers 76; **no smoking** verboden te roken

snacks 22,23

snake bite de slangenbeet

snow de sneeuw; ~ **chains** s- kettingen 71; **it's** ~**ing** het sneeuwt 95

soap de zeep 47; ~ **powder** het zeeppoeder 44

socket/s het stopcontact -*en* 17

sock/s de sok *sokken* 48

soft zacht; ~ **drink/s** de fris *frisdranken* 23,91

software de software 61

sole *fish* de tong 41

some wat 25,38; ~**one** iemand; ~**thing** iets 22; ~**times** soms

son/s de zoon -*s* 89,92

song/s het lied *liederen*

soon spoedig; **as** ~ **as possible** zo s- mogelijk 84

sorry! sorry!; **I'm** ~ het spijt me 12,57,132

sort: **what** ~ **of** wat voor 23,73

soup de soep 23

south zuid 64

spanner de (moer)sleutel 71

spark plug/s de kaars -*en*, de bougie -*s* 71

to **speak** spreken 56; *to* met; **I** ~ ik spreek 57,90,132; **you** ~ u spreekt 132

special: offer de aanbieding 49; **today's** ~ de dagschotel 22,27

speciality de specialiteit

spectacles de bril
speed limits 67
to spell spellen 57; how do you ~ hoe
spel je 54
spinach de spinazie 42
spoke/s de spaak *spaken* 71
spoon/s de lepel -s 18,19
sport de sport 86,91; ~s ground het
sportterein
spring de lente; in ~ in de lente 95
square *town* het plein 51; main ~
het marktplein
stairs de trap 16
is stalling slaat af 70 (stall afslaan)
stamp/s de postzegel -s 45,52
to stand staan 76
starboard stuurboord 78
to start starten 70,87
statement of account het
rekeninguittreksel 63
station/s het station -s 54,74-76
to stay *remain* blijven 7,20,90; *reside*
verblijven 93; wonen 90
steak de steak 27; de biefstuk -
stukken 40
to steal stelen; stolen gestolen 93
steam train de stoomtrein;
steamer de stoomboot
still nog
to sting steken; stung gestoken 82
stomach de maag 85; ~ ache de
maagpijn 46
stop/s de halte -n; *bus* bushalte 77
(to ~ stoppen)
stop! stop it! hou op! 93 (~ doing
ophouden)
stopcock de hoofdkraan 17
store/s de winkel -s 38-50
storey/s de verdieping -en 12,59
storm/s de storm -en; *gale warning*
de s-waarschuwing 79
stove *cooker* het fornuis 18
straight on rechtdoor 66
strap/s *luggage* de bagageriem -en
71
strawberries aardbeien 29,43
street/s de straat *straten* 66; main ~
de hoofds-; ~ map het
stratenplan 45
string het touw 45
strong sterk
it's stuck het zit vast 72
student/s de student -en 88,90
to study studeren
subsidiary company het
dochterbedrijf 62
subway *train* de metro 78
I suffer from ik lijd aan 84 (to ~
lijden)
sugar de suiker 44

to suggest voorstellen
suitcase/s de koffer -s
summer de zomer 95
sun de zon; ~burn de zonnebrand
46; ~glasses zonnebril 47;
sunny zonnig 95; ~tan cream
de zonnecrème 47
Sunday zondag 26,68,94; *(dates)* 59
supermarket de supermarkt 38
with supplement met toeslag 75
sure zeker 58
go surfling surfen; ~board de surfplank
86
surrounding area de omgeving
sweater/s de trui -en 48,49
sweetcorn de maïs 34,42
sweets bonbons, snoep
to swim zwemmen 86; ~ming
costume/trunks het zwempak/de
zwembroek 48; ~ming pool het
zwembad 86

T

table/s de tafel -s 19,26
to take nemen 50,66,83; *I'll have* ik
neem 27,57; ~ place 78; ~ with
you, etc meenemen; *sugar, etc*
gebruiken; *time* duren 15,78;
unoccupied vrij 22
to talk spreken 56,57; *to* met
tall hoog; *people* lang
tampon/s de tampon -s 47
tap/s de kraan -en 17
tape *sticky* het plakband
tarif het tarief 7,68
tart/s de taart -en
that tastes dit smaakt: bad vies 28; nice
lekker 91; *I don't like it* het
smaakt mij niet (taste smaken)
tax/es de belasting -en (13); before ~
netto prijs 63
taxi/s de taxi *taxi's* 54
tea de thee 23,25; ~pot de t-pot 19;
~spoon het t-lepeltje 19; ~ towel
de keukenhanddoek 19
teacher/s de leraar *leraren*
telephone/s de telefoon -s 53,56,61;
~ directory het t-boek; mobile ~
de GSM 57; ~ number het t-
nummer 57; phone card de t-
kaart 53; zone no. het
netnummer (to ~ bellen 54)
to tell zeggen 77
temperature *fever* de koorts 82,84
ten tien 131
tennis het tennis; play ~ tennissen
86; ~ ball, racket de bal, het
racket 86
tent/s de tent -en 7,20
tetanus tetanus 82

than dan

thankl **you** dank u 132; **many ~s**
hartelijk dank 61; **~s for your
help** dank for uw hulp 14; *don't
mention it* niets te danken, tot uw
dienst 57 (**to ~** danken)

that dat 21,38; die 24,38; **that's all**
dat is alles 39; **~ one** dat daar;
one like ~ zo een 29,39

the de, het 70,96

theatre/s het theater *-s* 87

theft 93

their hun 97

them hun/ze

then dan 21

there daar 66; **over ~** ginds 51

there is/are er is/zijn 17,132; **~ is no**
er is geen 17 *(be* zijn 97)

they zij/ze 97

thick dik

thing/s het ding *-en*

thin mager

to **think** denken, vinden; **I ~ so** dat denk
ik; **I don't...** dat denk ik niet; **do
you ~ so** vindt u 90,91/ vind je;
do (don't) you ~ so vindt u (niet)

I'm **thirsty** ik heb dorst 22 (**be ~** dorst
hebben)

this, ~ one, these deze 24,38,49; dit
15,28,89

thread het garen 45

three drie 20

throat de keel 85; **sore ~** de k-pijn
46

through door

Thursday donderdag 68,94; *(dates)*
59

ticket/s *buying* 76,78,80; *(spoken)*
het kaartje *-s* 77,87, *(written)* de
kaart *-en* 74; **all-day ~** de
dagkaart 68; **~ machine** de
automaat 68,74; **~ office** het
loket 74; **strip ~** de strippenkaart
75,77; *entertainment* 87; *flight*
het ticket 80; *stamping* 75

tide/s het tij *-en* 79; **low and high ~**
ebbe en vloed 79

tights de nylons 48

tile/s de tegel *-s* 14

time de tijd 21,**55**,59,68,87; **~s a day**
maal per dag 84; **~s of day** 94

timetable/s de dienstregeling *-en* 75

tin/s het blik *blikken;* **~ opener** de
blikopener 45

tipping 22,54

tired moe; **I'm ~** ik ben moe

to **naar** 54,76, aan; *until* tot 13; **in
order ~** om te; **to the** ten; *with
verb* 97

toast de toast 25

today vandaag 15,74; **~'s special** de
dagschotel 22,27

toe/s de teen *tenen*

together samen 59

toilet de WC 10,24,66; **~ paper** het
WC papier 44; *Ladies* Dames,
Mens Heren 66

toiletries 47

tomato/es de tomaat *tomaten* 38,42

tomorrow morgen 15,87,94; **~
morning** m-ochtend

tonight vannacht 21; *this evening*
vanavond 87,90

too te 49

tools 70-71

toothl**ache** de kiespijn 84; **~brush**
de tandenborstel 47; **~paste** de
tandpasta 47

torch de zaklantaarn 45

total het totaal 63

tour/s de rondrit *-ritten;* **guided ~** de
rondleiding *-en* (88)

tourist/s de toerist *-en;* **~ office** de
VVV *(NL),* het bureau voor
toerisme *(B)* 65,**88**

to **tow** slepen; **~ away** wegslepen

towards naar

tower/s de toren *-s*

towel/s de handdoek *-en* 16; **tea ~**
de keukenh- 19

town/s de stad *steden* 64,88; **~
centre** het stadscentrum 65; **~
hall** het stadhuis; **home ~** de
woonplaats; **~ square** het plein
51

toys het speelgoed; **a toy** een stuk s-

traffic het verkeer; **~ jam** de file 67;
~ lights de verkeerslichten 66;
through ~ doorgaand v- 67;
priority 67,69

train/s de trein *-en* 74-76; **express ~**
sneltrein 75; **go by ~** met de
trein gaan; **local ~** stoptrein 75;
underground ~ de metro 78

tram/s de tram *-s* 67,**77**; **~ stop** de
tramhalte

transfer *money* transfer maken 63;
trains etc overstappen 76

to **translate** vertalen

trash het vuilnis 18; **~ can** de v-bak;
~ collection de v-omhaling 14

to **travel** reizen; **~ bureau** het
reisbureau; **~ sickness** de
reisziekte 46; **~ler's cheque** de
reischeque 50,51,93

tree/s de boom *bomen*

trip/s reis *reizen* 78; **round ~** de
rondvaart, *ticket* heen en terug
76; **have a good ~** prettige reis!
67

tripe de ingewanden 40
trousers de broek 48
trout de forel *forellen* 41
true waar; **that's ~** dat is w-
to **try** proberen; **~ on** aanpassen 49
T-shirt/s de T-shirt *-s* 48
Tuesday dinsdag 68,94; *(dates)* 59
tulip/s de tulp *-en*
tuna de tonijn 41
tunnel/s de tunnel *-s* 64; **Channel T-** de Kanaaltunnel
turkey/s de kalkoen *-en* 40
to **turn** draaien; **~ off** draai dicht, *on* open 17
turnover de jaaromzet 63
TV de televisie, tv 18; **~ aerial** de televisieantenne 18
two twee 10,131; *second* tweede 59; *twice* tweemaal
to **type** typen; **have s.t. typed** ... laten typen 61
tyre/s de band *-en* 71; **~ pressure** de b-druk 71,72

U

you u 97
umbrella/s de paraplu *paraplu's*
uncle/s de oom *-s*
under onder
underground *train* de metro 78
underpants de herenslip 48
understand: I don't ~ ik begrijp het niet; **do you ~** begrijpt u 132; *(know s.t.)* verstaan (ik versta)
unemployed werkloos
unfortunately jammer genoeg
unit/s de eenheid *eenheden* 53
university -ties de universiteit *-en*
unlimited onbeperkt 73 *(to limit -* beperken)
unmarried ongetrouwd
until tot; **not ~** pas
upstairs boven
urgent dringend 81,84
urine de urine; **~ sample** het u- staal 83
USA de Verenigde Staten, de V.S. 52,92
us ons
to **use** gebruiken 61, *be equipped with* beschikken over 7; **for external ~** voor uitwendig gebruik; **useful** nuttig
usual/ly gewoonlijk; **as ~** als g-

V

vacant vrij 9,24,66
vacation de vakantie; **I'm on ~** ik ben met v-
vaccinated against gevaccineerd tegen 82

vacuum cleaner de stofzuiger 18
valid geldig 74; **to be ~ for** gelden voor 68
valley/s de vallei *-en* 64
valve/s de klep *kleppen* 71
vanilla vanille 29
VAT BTW 13,22,63
veal het kalfsvlees 33,40
vegetable/s de groente *-n* 24,32,42
vegetarian/s *person* de vegetariër *-s* 28,30; *food* vegetarisch 28,30
very zeer; erg 14,27
via over
video de video 18
village/s het dorp *-en*
vinegar de azijn
visit het bezoek 90,(**91**); **~ors** bezoekers 68; **address for ~ors** het bezoekadres (**to ~** bezoeken)
to **vomit** overgeven 82

W

waffel/s de wafel *-s* 22
to **wait** wachten 56; **~ a minute** wacht eens; **~ for** wachten op; **~ing room** de wachtkamer 75
Wales Wales, **Welsh** Welsh/Welshe *m/f* 92
walk/s de wandeling *-en* 88; **I ~** ik loop 67 (**to ~** lopen)
wall/s de muur *muren* 14
wallet de portefeuille
to **want** willen 97; **I ~** ik wil 26,36,76,91,132; **I ~ed** ik wilde 97; **do you ~** wilt u 20,76
warm warm; **~er** warmer 17, 95; *hearty* hartelijk 14
I **was** ik was
to **wash** wassen; **~basin** de wastafel 17; **~ing machine** de wasmachine 18; **~ing up liquid** het afwasproduct 44
wasp/s de wesp *-en*
water het water 17,29,79; **~ heater** de w-verwarmer 17; **~ melon** de w-meloen 43; **~ skiing** w-skiën 86
way: finding the ~ 66; **~ in** de ingang; **~ out** de uitgang 74,88
WC de WC 10,24,66
we wij, we 7,23,25,97
weather het weer 95; **~ forecast** de w-svoorspelling 79
Wednesday woensdag 68,94; *(dates)* 59
week/s de week *weken* 9,68,73,94; **~days** werkdagen 75; **~end** het weekeinde
weight het gewicht
welcome: you're ~ niets te danken; *at your service* tot uw dienst 57

well-known bekend
well-done *food* doorgebakken 27
I **went** ik ging 97 *(go* gaan 97)
west west 64
wet nat
what wat 93; ~ **did you say** w- zei u
132; ~ **is it** hoe heet dit 24; ~
kind of w- voor 23,73; ~ **time is
it** hoe laat is het; ~ **would you
like** w- wilt u 25,91
wheat de tarwe
wheel/s het wiel *-en* 71; ~**chair** de
rolstoel 7; ~**chair facilities**
rolstoelfaciliteiten
when? wanneer? 15,57,77; **when...**
als...
where waar 14,79; ~ **from** w-
vandaan 78,90; ~ **is** w- is
66,132; ~ **to** w-...naar toe 76
which welk 49,76,96; **in** ~ waarin
Whit. Monday 2e Pinksterdag 75
white wit fc,29
whiting de wijting 41
who wie 57,132; **whose** van w-; **to
whom** aan w-
whole heel; **the** ~ **day** de gehele dag
why waarom
wide breed/brede
wife *wives* de vrouw *-en* 89
that **will** dat zal 54
wind de wind 79; ~**mill**/s de w-molen
-s 64; ~**surfing** w-surfen 86; **it's
windy** het waait 95
window/s het venster *-s* 16, het raam
ramen
windI**screen/shield** de voorruit 71; ~
wipers de ruitenwissers 71
wine/s de wijn *-en* 29,91
winter de winter 95
wishes: best ~ met vriendelijke
groeten
with met 10,50
without zonder; *salted only* 22

woman/women de vrouw *-en; Ladies'*
Dames 66
wonderful prachtig, prima
wood het bos 65
wool de wol
word/s het woord *-en;* **in other** ~**s**
m.a.w. *(met andere woorden)*
work het werk 90; *unemployed*
werkloos
to **work** werken (90; ik werk); **doesn't** ~
werkt niet 15,70
write: **can you** ~ **it down** kunt u dat
opschrijven 132; **in writing**
schriftelijk 63 (**to** ~ schrijven; ik
schrijf)
wrong: **that's** ~ dat is verkeerd; *bill*
het klopt niet 28

Y

yacht/s het jacht *-en* 79; *marina* de j-
haven 78
yard/s de tuin *-en* 14
year/s, **years old** het jaar *jaren*
63,83; **Happy New** ~ Gelukkig
Nieuwjaar 95
yellow geel fc
yes ja 8,132; ~ **indeed** jawel; ~ **of
course** jazeker 9
yesterday gisteren 94
not **yet** nog niet
yogurt de yoghurt 44
you u *polite* 51,91,97; jij/jullie *fam.
s/pl* 89,90,91,97
young jong; ~ **person** de jonge
your uw 8,51,97; ~**s
faithfully/sincerely** hoogachtend
7
youth hostel de jeugdherberg 21; ~
manager de huisbewaarder 21

Z

zoo de dierentuin
zucchini courgettes 42

Numbers

0	nul *nuwl*	17	zeventien *zayvuhteen*	1000	duizend *duh(oo)zent*
1	een *ayn*	18	achttien *akhtteen*	1001	duizend één *duh(oo)zent ayn*
2	twee *tvay*	19	negentien *naykhuhteen*	1100	elfhonderd *elf hondert*
3	drie *dree*	20	**twin**tig *tvintukh*	2000	tweeduizend *tvay duh(oo)zent*
4	vier *veer*	21	eenentwintig *aynuntvintukh*	1.000.000	miljoen *milyoon*
5	vijf *vayf*	22	tweeëntwintig *tvayuntvintukh*		
6	zes *zess*	30	**der**tig *dairtukh*	1960	negentien zestig
7	zeven *zayvuh*	40	**veer**tig *vayrtukh*	2002	tweeduizend twee
8	acht *akht*	50	vijftig *vayftukh*	1. (1ste)	**eerste** 1st *ayrstuh*
9	negen *naykhuh*	60	zestig *zestukh*	2. (2de)	tweede 2nd *tvayduh*
10	tien *teen*	70	zeventig *zayvuhtukh*	3. (3de)	**der**de 3rd *dairduh*
11	elf *elf*	80	**t**achtig *takhtukh*	1 1/2	anderhalf
12	twaalf *tvaalf*	90	negentig *naykhuhtukh*		
13	**der**tien *dairteen*	100	honderd *hondert*		
14	**veer**tien *vayrteen*	101	honderd één *hondert ayn*		
15	vijftien *vayfteen*	121	honderd eenentwintig *hondert aynuntvintukh*		
16	zestien *zesteen*	200	tweehonderd *tvay hondert*	NB 1,5 één komma vijf = 1.5 Du. 6 : 3 = En. 6 ÷ 3 = 2

Yes.	Ja.	*ya*
No.	Nee.	*nay*
Please.	Alsjeblieft.	*ashoo-**bleeft***
Thank you.	Dank u.	*dankoo*
Thank you very much.	Hartelijk dank.	***har**tuh-luk dank*

OK.	OK	*okay*
You're welcome.	Tot uw dienst.	***tott**uw **deenst***
Excuse me.	Pardon.	*per-**don***
Sorry!	Sorry!	*sorry*
I'm sorry.	Het spijt me.	*hut **spayt**-muh*

Hello.	Dag.	*dakh*
Good morning.	Goedemorgen.	***hooyuh morkhuh***
Good evening.	Goedenavond.	***hooyuh aavont***
Goodbye. See you soon.	Da-ag. Tot ziens.	*dakh. tot seenss*
How are you?	Hoe gaat het?	*hoo **khaat**-hut?*
Fine thanks - and you?	Goed dank u. En met u?	***khoot** dankoo. en met **oo**?*

How much is it?	Hoeveel is het?	*hoo-vayl iss-hut?*
I'd like ...	Graag ...	*hraakh ...*
We'd like ...	We willen graag ...	*vuh villuh hraakh ...*
There is/are ...	Er is/zijn ...	*er iss/zayn ...*
Is/are there ...?	Is/zijn er ...?	*iss/zayn er ... ?*
Can one/may we ...?	Mag ik/mogen we ... ?	***makh**-ik/**moakh**uh-vuh ...?*

When?	Wanneer?	*van-**ayr**?*
Where?	Waar?	*vaar?*
Who?	Wie?	*vee?*

Do you speak English?	Spreekt u Engels?	*spraykt-oo **eng**-elss?*
I don't speak Dutch.	Ik spreek geen Nederlands.	*ik sprayk khayn **nay**derlants*
Do you understand?	Begrijpt u?	*buh-**khraypt**-oo?*
I don't understand.	Ik begrijp het niet.	*ik buh-**khrayp** hut **neet***
I don't know.	Ik weet het niet.	*ik **vayt** hut neet*

| What did you say? | Wat zei u? | *vat zay oo?* |

Could you speak more slowly, please?	Kunt u langzamer spreken, a.u.b.?	***kun**too **lang**zaamer spraykuh, ashoo-**bleeft**?*
Can you repeat that?	Kunt u dat herhalen?	***kun**too dat her-**haaluh**?*
Can you write it down?	Kunt u dat opschrijven?	***kun**too dat **ops**khray-vuh?*

Can you help me?	Kunt u me helpen?	***kun**too-muh helpuh?*
I'm lost.	Ik ben de weg kwijt.	*ik benduh **vekh kvayt***
I've lost ...	Ik ben ... kwijt.	*ik ben ... **kvayt***
What's the matter?	Wat is er aan de hand?	*vat **isser** aanduh hant?*
It doesn't matter.	Dat geeft niet.	*dat **khayft** neet*